T0022829

Is the American Century Over?

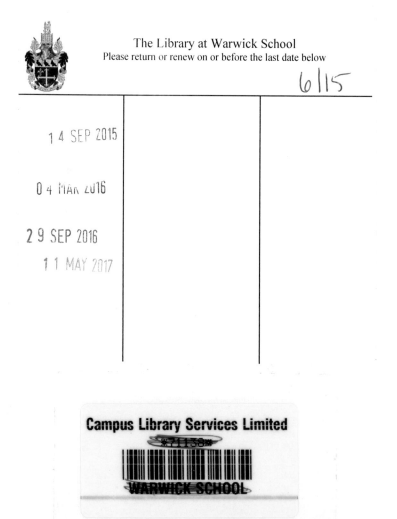

The Library at Warwick School
Please return or renew on or before the last date below

6/15

1 4 SEP 2015		
0 4 MAR 2016		
2 9 SEP 2016		
1 1 MAY 2017		

Campus Library Services Limited

WARWICK SCHOOL

Global Futures Series

"The future of American power is the great question of our century. No one is better equipped than Joe Nye to answer it."

Lt. Gen. Brent Scowcroft, USAF (ret.) former Presidential National Security Advisor

"This calm, reflective, and thoughtful antidote to alarm about American decline displays Nye's astonishing capacity to engage with the full range of challenges to American leadership."

Michael Ignatieff, Harvard Kennedy School

"In this timely, compact book, Joe Nye makes a 'powerful' case for the continuation of American primacy through diplomacy and cooperation. This strategy would not be overstretch or retrenchment but instead the application of American exceptionalism to shrewd power."

Robert B. Zoellick, former President of the World Bank Group, US Trade Representative, and US Deputy Secretary of State

"The irreversibility of American decline is no longer a given. Joe Nye's compelling analysis shows that the future of the international order, and the respective roles of the US and China within it, will be shaped by a range of core domestic and foreign policy choices, rather than by some overwhelming, determinist, historical force that has somehow already decided the 'natural' dimensions, depth, and duration of American power. The history of nations, as Joe Nye rightly asserts, is a more dynamic process than that."

Kevin Rudd, former Prime Minister of Australia

"Joe Nye is always worth reading – objective without being aloof, insightful without lecturing. Our disordered world needs answers to the challenges posed here."

David Miliband, UK Foreign Secretary 2007–10

"Nye's masterful analysis shows the defenders of America's continued primacy how to make their most credible case while forcing the declinists to engage with its arguments, and even rethink their assumptions."

Amitav Acharya, American University, and author of
The End of American World Order

"In this tour de force, Joe Nye proves that smart books about big ideas are best served in small packages: and if you are looking for one volume to read on a topic about which so much nonsense has been written since the disaster that was the Bush administration, this is the one to go for. Balanced, accessible, informed – but above all, wise – Nye demonstrates once more why he continues to influence the way we all think about the world."

Michael Cox, LSE IDEAS

"Joe Nye's clear-eyed analysis makes a very compelling case that the 'American century' is far from over, even though, with a less preponderant America and a more complex world, its next chapter will look different. It's not the sexiest argument. But utterly convincing."

Wolfgang Ischinger, Chairman of the Munich Security Conference and former German Ambassador to the US

"With his usual clarity and insight, Joe Nye gives us a fascinating analysis of the complexities of power, exploring hard and soft power, state and non-state actors, and how to retain leadership once domination is over. European readers have much to learn from the US experience and its lessons for the evolution of the EU."

Mario Monti, Prime Minister of Italy (2011–13) and President of Bocconi University

Joseph S. Nye Jr.

———

Is the American Century Over?

polity

Copyright © Joseph S. Nye Jr. 2015

The right of Joseph S. Nye Jr. to be identified as Author of this Work has been asserted in accordance with the UK Copyright, Designs and Patents Act 1988.

First published in 2015 by Polity Press

Polity Press
65 Bridge Street
Cambridge CB2 1UR, UK

Polity Press
350 Main Street
Malden, MA 02148, USA

All rights reserved. Except for the quotation of short passages for the purpose of criticism and review, no part of this publication may be reproduced, stored in a retrieval system, or transmitted, in any form or by any means, electronic, mechanical, photocopying, recording or otherwise, without the prior permission of the publisher.

ISBN-13: 978-0-7456-9006-3
ISBN-13: 978-0-7456-9007-0(pb)

A catalogue record for this book is available from the British Library.

Is the American Century Over?
Library of Congress Cataloging in Publication Control Number: 2014036840

Typeset in 11 on 15 pt Sabon by
Servis Filmsetting Ltd, Stockport, Cheshire
Printed and bound in the United States by Edwards Brothers Malloy

The publisher has used its best endeavours to ensure that the URLs for external websites referred to in this book are correct and active at the time of going to press. However, the publisher has no responsibility for the websites and can make no guarantee that a site will remain live or that the content is or will remain appropriate.

Every effort has been made to trace all copyright holders, but if any have been inadvertently overlooked the publisher will be pleased to include any necessary credits in any subsequent reprint or edition.

For further information on Polity, visit our website:
politybooks.com

Contents

Acknowledgments

I want to thank Louise Knight of Polity Press for suggesting this short book as a way to summarize more than two decades of my thinking on this subject and bring it up to date for a general audience.

Robert O. Keohane, Strobe Talbott, and Ali Wyne provided helpful comments on an early draft. Inesha Premaratne was a wonderful research assistant, and Jeanne Marasca has been a fine general assistant for many years. I am grateful to my colleagues at The Center for Public Leadership and the Belfer Center for Science and International Affairs at the Harvard Kennedy School of Government for their support and intellectual stimulation, which I hope is reflected in these pages. Above all, I thank Molly Harding Nye not only for reading and commenting on the manuscript, but for providing the life support that makes everything possible.

Acknowledgments

No author is an island. I have had the benefit of learning from many people as I have lived through the American century. To them all, I am grateful.

1

The Creation of the American Century

Is the American century over? Many seem to think so. In recent years, polls showed that in 15 of 22 countries surveyed, most respondents said that China either will replace or has already replaced the United States as the world's leading power. A Pew poll in 2014 found only 28 percent of Americans thought their country "stands above all others" compared to 38 percent in 2011. Yet perhaps, as Mark Twain famously quipped, "reports of my death have been greatly exaggerated."

After American independence in the eighteenth century, the British politician Horace Walpole lamented that Britain had been reduced to the level of Sardinia. In fact, Britain was about to be transformed by the industrial revolution that created its second century as a global power. In the mid-1980s, an MIT economist asked why, if the British empire attraction and persuasion are called soft power. All these dimensions of power are important, and that is why economic power alone should not be used to define the American century. For example, when the United States became the largest economy at the end of the nineteenth century, it was not regarded as a major player in the global balance of power until Presidents Theodore Roosevelt and Woodrow Wilson invested some of that economic power into military resources. Moreover, even when a country has major power resources, it may have a poor power conversion capability, as the United States demonstrated in the 1930s when it had the largest economy but followed an isolationist policy. So when China passes the United States in total economic size, we will not automatically be witnessing the end of the American century if we consider all three dimensions of economic, military, and soft power. (Moreover, as we will see below, the total size of GDP is only one aspect of economic power.)

A more useful way of defining and dating the American century is not only in terms of power resources, but also in terms of the ways in which the United States used those resources to affect the global balance of power.[5] In the nineteenth century, the Americans used their economic power to trade with the rest of the world, but played a small role in the global balance of power. Following George Washington's advice to avoid entangling alliances and the Monroe Doctrine, which focused on the Western hemisphere, the United States played only a minor role in the global balance. The United States did not keep a large standing army, and in 1880s the US navy was smaller than that of Chile. The Americans did not shun military power (as Mexico and native American nations can attest), but isolationism described the US attitude toward the European great powers. In the short Spanish-American war of 1898, the United States took the colonies of Cuba, Puerto Rico, and the Philippines from a declining Spain; but that period of formal global imperialism was brief. While Theodore Roosevelt built up the American navy and dabbled in global diplomacy, American foreign policy remained primarily focused on the Western hemisphere.

A big change was American entry into World War I. Michael Lind recently argued:

[I]n 1914, the American Century began. This year the American Century ended. America's foreign policy is in a state of collapse, America's economy doesn't work well, and American democracy is broken. The days when other countries looked to the U.S. as a successful model of foreign policy prudence, democratic capitalism and liberal democracy may be over. The American Century, 1914–2014. RIP.[6]

Leaving hyperbole aside, in 1917 Woodrow Wilson broke with tradition and for the first time sent American troops to fight in Europe. Moreover, he proposed a League of Nations to organize collective security on a global basis. After the Senate rejected American membership in the League and the troops came home, America "returned to normal." Though it was now a major factor in the global power balance, the United States became virulently isolationist in the 1930s. Thus it would be more accurate to date the American century with Franklin Roosevelt's entry into World War II. It was in this context, to resist isolationism and urge American participation in the war, that Henry Luce, the son of missionary parents, wrote his famous February 1941 editorial on "the American Century" in *LIFE* magazine.[7]

Equally important were Harry Truman's postwar decisions that led to a permanent military presence abroad. When Britain was too weak to support Greece and Turkey in 1947, the United States took its place. It invested heavily in the Marshall Plan in 1948, created NATO in 1949, and led a United

Nations coalition that fought in Korea in 1950. These actions were part of the strategy of containment. As the diplomat George Kennan (and others) saw the world after World War II, there were five main areas of industrial productivity and strength: the United States, the Soviet Union, Britain, Europe, and Japan. It was in the American interest to ally with three of the five as a means of containing the growth of Soviet power. American troops remain in Europe, Japan , Korea and elsewhere to this day.

From 1945 to 1991, the global balance of power was described as bipolar, with two superpowers standing well above the rest. The United States and the Soviet Union had disproportionate shares of power resources, alliance spheres of influence, and competed for advantage in the non-aligned world. The two giants engaged in a nuclear arms race, and balanced each other's power. But after the fall of the Berlin Wall in 1989 and the collapse of the Soviet Union (primarily because of internal reasons) in 1991, the United States become the world's only superpower.

Though the terminology is unfortunate, theorists of international relations called this a "unipolar" world. Some might say that 1991 is a third potential date for the beginning of the American century, when the United States became the only nation able to project military power on a global scale. The American navy was equal in size to the next 17 navies, American forces had air superiority, the United States took the lead in space and cyber space, and the US military budget represented nearly half the global total. In such circumstances, it became very difficult for other states to form coalitions that could balance American military power.

Myths of American hegemony

No other state in modern history has had as much military preponderance as the United States. Some analysts call this American "hegemony" and compare it to British hegemony in the nineteenth century. It is common to hear that the United States "appears to be following in the footsteps of Great Britain, the last global hegemon."[8] The historical analogy is popular, but misleading.

During the so-called *Pax Britannica*, Britain was not as preponderant as the United States is today. British policy was to maintain a navy equal to the next two fleets combined, and Britain had an empire on which the sun never set, and ruled over a quarter of humankind. Nonetheless, there were major differences in the relative power resources of imperial Britain and contemporary America. By the time of World War I, Britain ranked only fourth among the great powers in its share of military personnel, fourth in GDP, and third in military spending.[9] The costs of defense averaged 2.5 to 3.4 percent of GDP and the empire was ruled in large part through local troops. Of the 8.6 million British forces in World War I, nearly a third came from the overseas empire.[10] But with the rise of nationalism, it became increasingly difficult for London to declare war on behalf of the empire, and by the time of World War II, protecting the empire became more of a burden than an asset. For all the loose talk of American empire, the United States has more degrees of freedom than Britain had. And while Britain faced powerful neighbors in Germany and Russia, America benefits from two oceans and weaker neighbors.

Moreover, the word "hegemony" is used in diverse and confusing ways. There is no general agreement on how much inequality and what types of power resources constitute hegemony. Some writers use the word "hegemonic" interchangeably with "imperial," but formal empire is not a requirement for hegemony. Others call it the ability to "order the international system," but argue that it has rarely existed.[11] Still others use the term as synonymous with primacy or having the most power resources, and refer to nineteenth-century Britain as hegemonic even though Britain ranked third (behind the United States and Russia) in GDP, and third (behind Russia and France) in military expenditures even at the height of its power in 1870. While Britain had a preponderant role in naval affairs, its power was balanced in other domains. Similarly, those who speak of American hegemony after 1945 fail to note that American military power was balanced by the Soviet Union for more than four decades. The Americans had disproportionate power in the world economy, but their political and military actions were constrained by Soviet power.

Some scholars have described the post-1945 period as an American-led hierarchical order with liberal characteristics, where weaker states were given institutional access to the exercise of American power, and the United States provided public goods and operated within a loose system of multilateral rules and institutions. As John Ikenberry describes it, "the United States provided global services – such as security protection and support of open markets – which made other states willing to work with rather than resist American pre-eminence."[12] Some analysts point out that it can be rational for states that benefit to preserve this institutional framework even if American power resources decline.[13] In that sense, the American century could outlive American primacy in power resources. Others argue that this open liberal institutional order is now coming to an end as new powers emerge.

Critics point out that there has always been a lot of fiction mixed with the facts in the mythology of American hegemony.[14] It was never really a global order, but more a group of like-minded states centered primarily in the Americas and Western Europe, and it did not always have benign effects on non-members. As Henry Kissinger notes, no truly global world order has ever existed.[15] Since the largest countries in the world – China, India, Indonesia, and the Soviet Bloc – were not members, the American world order was really less than half the world. In terms of the global military balance, the United States was not hegemonic. In economics, American leadership created liberal institutions and rules and practices that governed the world economy, but for only half the world. It might, more accurately, be called a "half-hegemony."

A Norwegian scholar, Geir Lundestad, once categorized this partial American world order after 1945 as an "empire by invitation," and its proponents have argued that by fostering multilateral institutions and allowing access to power for other states, the Americans legitimized a liberal order that in principle could survive the gradual decline of the United States. Can China, India, Brazil, and other emerging powers be co-opted into this order? Among others, Amitav Acharya thinks not, and he foresees a world order based on regionalism and plural narratives. He offers the metaphor of a multiplex cinema theater where, rather than one film playing, there will be many equal choices under a common architecture. "Hence, instead of pining for the American-led liberal hegemonic order, we should prepare to 'boldly go where no-one has gone before.'"[16]

Half-hegemony

As we have seen, the term "hegemony" is too imprecise a concept to be useful in defining "the American century." Sometimes it means having a preponderance of power resources, sometimes the behavior of setting the rules for others, and some-times getting the outcomes one prefers. Because of this ambiguity, we cannot date when it begins or ends. Noam Chomsky even argues that the "'loss of China' was the first major step in 'America's decline,'" or about the time that many others see ascendance.[17] If there ever was a US hegemony, it would have been from 1945, when the United States had nearly half the world economy as a result of World War II, to 1970, when the US share of world product declined to its pre-war level of a quarter of world product. Yet during this period, the United States often failed to get what it wanted – witness Soviet acquisition of nuclear weapons; communist takeover of China and half of Vietnam; stalemate in the Korean War; Soviet suppression of the revolts in Hungary and Czechoslovakia; Castro's control of Cuba; and so forth. Thus, instead of "hegemony," I prefer to use the terms "primacy" or "preeminence" in terms of a country's disproportionate (and measurable) share of all three types of power resources.

After 1945, the United States had preeminence in economic power resources, but in the political-military dimensions of power, the world was bipolar rather than "hegemonic," and the Soviet Union balanced American power. Unipolarity did not come until the collapse of the USSR in 1991. As for being a benign hegemon providing public goods, the American world order did provide shared goods such as security and prosperity for parts of the world, but these were club goods available to members rather than global public goods. For many non-members of the club, such as India, China, Indonesia, Congo, Iran, Guatemala, and Chile, among others, the measures taken to provide security and prosperity for members of the club did not look like benign public goods. Because of these ambiguities in the concept of hegemony, it is better to define "the American century" as the period since the beginning of World War II, when the United States, without full control, had primacy in economic power resources and became a central actor in the global balance of power. Thus, "the American century" – date of birth: 1941; date of death: uncertain.

The short answer to our question is that we are not entering a post-American world. It is not possible for this (or any) book to see "the future," because there are so many possible futures dependent on unpredictable events and they play a larger role the further out one tries to look. Thus it is important to specify a time horizon. For example, if the "American century" began in 1941, will the United States still have primacy in power resources and play the central role in the global balance of power among states in 2041? My guess is "yes." In that sense, the American century is not over, but because of transnational and non-state forces, it is definitely changing in important ways that are described below. But first, we must look at the charge that the United States is in decline.

2

American Decline?

It goes against common sense and history to believe that the United States will have a dominant share of world power forever. But what is the life cycle of a country? Political entities are social constructs without clear lifespans, unlike human organisms where a century is generally the limit (though science will eventually extend this somewhat.) When you look at persons, you can generally judge whether they are in decline, though that depends on what functions you focus on – for example, athletic skill vs. mental acuity. The evidence about nations is harder to measure, and the time horizons may be much longer. Rome reached its apogee in AD 117, but the Western Roman empire did not collapse until some three and a half centuries later, and the Eastern Roman empire persisted until 1453.

American Decline?

Lessons from history

Despite such problems, some analysts and historians have tried to discern century-long patterns in the life cycles of dominant countries. In 1919, the British geo-politician Sir Halford Mackinder argued that unequal growth among nations tends to produce a hegemonic world war about every 100 years. More recently, political scientist George Modelski proposed a 100-year-long cycle of change in world leadership, starting with a major war and the power of the victor subsequently legitimized by postwar peace treaties that are eventually challenged and decay. He portrays Portugal as being preponderant from 1516 to 1540; the Netherlands from 1609 to 1640; Britain twice, from 1714 to 1740 and again from 1815 to 1850; and the United States dominant after the global wars of 1914–45 until decline set in in 1973.[1]

Immanuel Wallerstein, a neo-Marxist analyst, depicts a period of Dutch hegemony consolidated in the Thirty Years' War followed by the onset of decline in 1650; British hegemony starting with the Napoleonic wars at the beginning of the nineteenth century and decline commencing at the end of the century; and American hegemony beginning with the twentieth-century world wars and decline commencing in 1967.[2] Both these schemes use the world wars as dates for the beginning of the American era, but both misinterpreted the 1945–70 decline of America's share of world product as a long-term trend rather than a cyclical "return to normal." Thus both schemes have a hard time explaining the fact that the United States, supposedly in decline, was the world's only superpower by the end of the century.

Many other schemes have been proposed, but all the grand theories of hegemony and decline suffer from vague definitions and conceptual Procrustean beds which cut or stretch history in strange ways. Trying to identify a nation with a century is always a somewhat arbitrary construct. History does not repeat itself. Mark Twain quipped that sometimes it rhymes, but we should be wary of rhymes that are mostly echoes in our minds.

Americans have a long history of worrying about their decline. Shortly after the founding of the Massachusetts Bay colony in the seventeenth century, some Puritans lamented a decline from earlier virtue. In the eighteenth century, the founding fathers focused on the history of Rome, and worried about the decline of the new American republic. In the nineteenth century, Charles Dickens observed that if you listen to its citizens, America always "is depressed, and always is stagnated, and always is in an alarming crisis, and never was otherwise."[3]

The political scientist Samuel P. Huntington identified five phases of declinism in the late twentieth century: after the USSR launched the first satellite in 1957; after President Nixon's announcement of multipolarity in the late 1960s; after the Arab oil embargo of 1973; after Soviet expansion in the late 1970s; and after the onset of President Reagan's fiscal and trade deficits in the late 1980's.[4] In this century, one must add the period after the financial crisis and great recession of 2008. According to a 2002 Pew poll about America's place in the world, 55 percent of Americans felt the United States was more important and powerful than it had been a decade earlier, while only 17 percent stated the contrary. By 2013, those numbers had almost exactly reversed.[5] As James Fallows points out, only with America's emergence as a global power after World War II did the idea of American "decline" routinely involve falling behind someone else. Before that, it meant falling short of expectations – God's, the Founders', posterity's – or of the previous virtues of America in its lost, great days.[6]

These episodes tell us more about popular psychology than geo-political analysis, but they also show how the idea of decline touches a raw nerve in American politics. The issue leads to countless charges and denials in the daily game of partisan politics. This would not matter much if it merely contributed to self-correcting efforts at improvement, as Huntington believed, but sometimes anxiety about decline can lead toward nationalistic and protectionist policies that do harm. Conversely, periods of hubris such as 2002 can lead to damage from over-extended policies such as the US invasion of Iraq in March 2003. There is no virtue in either understatement or overstatement of American power.

Before looking at whether the United States is in "decline," it is important to note that the word is ambiguous and bundles together two quite different concepts: a decrease in relative external power, and domestic deterioration or decay. The first is relative decline and the second is absolute decline. While the two are often related, they need not be. In the seventeenth century, Spain declined externally because of internal economic problems. In contrast, the Dutch economy flourished, but the Netherlands experienced external relative decline simply because other countries (like Britain) were becoming stronger. And the Republic of Venice, which suffered external decline when trade routes in the Adriatic shifted, nonetheless continued its cultural progress. The Western half of the Roman empire was not the victim of a rising challenger state, but of long-term pressure of invading migratory tribes, each of which was weaker than Rome. Civic corruption, internecine warfare and loss of administrative and military efficiency allowed weak nomadic tribes to sack Rome. Domestic absolute decline meant Rome lost the capacity to convert its power resources into effective behavioral power.

What about the decline of the British empire? The fact that an island the size of a middling American state came to rule a quarter of the globe reflected Britain's position at the first wave of the industrial revolution in an era before the global spread of nationalism. Nonetheless, it was a remarkable conversion of domestic power resources into external expansion. By 1900, many people were worried about Britain's ability to sustain its position. The American writer Brooks Adams described what he saw as a loss of British vitality because of high living and the unwillingness to accept casualties in the Boer War. This was disproved by the enormous casualties Britain was willing to suffer in World War I. Britain emerged with the largest air force and navy and its empire at maximum size, but external factors such as the 30-year struggle with Germany, the rise of new naval powers like the United States and Japan, and the growth of nationalism in the empire reduced Britain's relative power. There were also signs of absolute internal decline, such as the failure to maintain the productivity of British industry, particularly in new sectors like chemicals and electricity, and an educational system that valued a classical training over science and technology skills for colonial rulers. Successful entrepreneurs sought entry into the landed classes rather than continuing as serial entrepreneurs, and the massive export of capital (over 8 per cent of net national product) proved a mixed blessing as Britain underinvested at home. But Britain's main problem was relative decline. British power could have survived the domestic problems had it not been for the rise of other powers. Before we look at America's domestic problems, it is important to ask about relative decline and which other states might challenge the United States.

3

Challengers and Relative Decline

Even if the United States is not in absolute decline, the American century may end simply because of the rise of others. Another country may become stronger than the United States, as Britain became more powerful than a prospering Netherlands in the seventeenth century. At the end of the nineteenth century, the simultaneous rise of Germany and Russia in Europe, Japan in the Pacific, and the United States in the Western hemisphere led Britain to accommodate the United States on various issues and restrict its naval doctrine (maintaining a navy larger than the next two combined) to waters near Europe. No one country may surpass the United States, but alliances among other states may put an end to American pre-eminence and its ability to maintain an international order. Are there plausible candidates for such roles?

Europe

When it acts as an entity, Europe is the largest economy in the world. Although the American economy is four times larger than Germany's, the total GDP of the European Union is slightly larger than that of the United States, and Europe's population of nearly 500 million is considerably larger than America's 310 million. American per capita income is higher than that of the EU, but in terms of human capital, technology, and exports, Europe is very much an economic peer competitor for the United States. Until the crisis of 2010, when fiscal problems in Greece and elsewhere created anxiety in financial markets, some economists speculated that the Euro might soon replace the dollar as the world's primary reserve currency.

In terms of military resources, Europe spends less than half of what the United States does on defense, but has more men under arms. Britain and France possess nuclear arsenals, and a limited capacity for overseas intervention in Africa and the Middle East. In soft power, European cultures have long had a wide appeal in the rest of the world, and the sense of a Europe uniting around Brussels had a strong attraction for its neighbors, though this was eroded somewhat after the financial crisis. Europeans have also played central roles in international institutions. The key question in assessing Europe's power resources is whether the EU will develop enough political and social-cultural cohesion to act as one on a wide range of international issues, or whether it will remain a limited grouping of countries with different nationalisms, political cultures, and foreign policies.

Europe's power conversion capability – or what Francis Fukuyama has called the discount rate between resources and outcomes – is limited, and it varies with different issues. On questions of trade and influence within the World Trade Organization, Europe is the equal of the United States and able to balance American power. Europe's role in the International Monetary Fund is second only to that of the United States (though the financial crisis dented confidence in the Euro.) On anti-trust issues, the size and attraction of the European market has meant that American firms seeking to merge have had to seek approval from the European Commission as well as the US Justice Department. In the cyber world, the EU is setting the global standards for privacy protection which multinational companies cannot ignore.

At the same time, Europe faces significant limits on its degree of unity. Although some young people identify primarily as Europeans, national identities remain stronger than a common European identity, as elections for the European Parliament have demonstrated. European institutions are unlikely to produce a strong federal Europe or a single state. None of this is to belittle European institutions and what they have accomplished. Legal integration is increasing, and European Court verdicts have compelled member countries to change policies. On the other hand, legislative and executive branch integration has lagged, and, while Europe has created a president and a central figure for foreign relations, the integration of foreign and defense policy is still limited. European nations may not be in one boat, but the ways the national boats are lashed together is historically unique.

While Europe is always changing, it is unlikely to surpass the United States. Europe faces serious demographic problems, both in birth rates and in political acceptance of immigrants. At its heyday in 1900, Europe accounted for a quarter of the world's population. By 2060, it may account for just 6 percent – and almost a third of these will be over 65 years. In terms of military expenditure, Europe is second only to the United States, with 15 percent of the world total (compared to 11 percent for China and 5 percent for Russia), but the number is misleading because Europe lacks military integration. In terms of economic power, Europe has the world's largest market and represents 17 percent of world trade compared to 12 percent for the United States. Europe dispenses half the world's foreign assistance, compared to 20 percent for the United States, but this has not produced much influence in distant regions like Asia. In terms of soft power, while Europe has 27 universities ranked in the top 100 (compared to 52 for the United States), the United States spends 2.7 per cent of GDP – twice as much as Europe – on universities and research and development. And while Europe's cultural industries are impressive, their size is less than that of their American counterparts. The EU's "creative industries" contributed about 7 percent to GDP, compared to 11 percent in the United States.[1] UNESCO found that in 2009, 14 out of the top 20 feature films were produced entirely in the United States; even in Europe, US motion pictures dominate the box office, accounting for 73 percent of revenue.[2]

If Europe were to overcome its internal differences and try to become a global challenger to the United States in a traditional balance of power, these assets might partly balance, but not equal, American power. On the other hand, if

Europe and America remain allied or even neutral, these resources could reinforce each other. Despite inevitable friction, economic separation is unlikely. Direct investment in both directions is higher than with Asia and helps knit the economies together. In addition, US–European trade is more balanced than US trade with Asia. At the cultural level, Americans and Europeans have sniped at each other for centuries, but they share values of democracy and human rights more with each other than with any other regions of the world. Neither the United States nor Europe is likely to threaten the vital or important interests of the other side. While political frictions will exist, the probability of a united Europe becoming more powerful than the United States and helping to cause the end of the American century is very low.

Japan

The same can be said for Japan. Three decades ago, many Americans feared being overtaken after Japanese per capita income surpassed that of the United States. Scholars predicted a Japanese-led Pacific bloc that would exclude the United States, and even an eventual war between Japan and the

United States. Some analysts forecast that Japan would become a nuclear superpower. Such views extrapolated from an impressive Japanese economic record, but today they simply remind us of the danger of linear projections based on rapidly rising economic growth rates.

Instead, Japan's economy suffered two decades of slow growth because of poor policy decisions that followed the bursting of a speculative bubble in the early 1990s. In 2010, China's economy passed Japan's in total size (measured in dollars), though it is only one-sixth of Japan's in per capita terms. Despite its recent performance, Japan retains impressive power resources, and the government of Prime Minister Shinzo Abe has taken policy steps to raise the rate of economic growth. Japan still possesses the world's third largest national economy, highly sophisticated industry, and the most modern military in Asia. While China has nuclear weapons and more men under arms, Japan's military is better equipped. It also has the technological capacity to develop nuclear weapons very quickly if it chooses to do so.

Japan faces severe demographic problems, with it population projected to shrink from today's 127 million to under 100 million by 2050, and its culture is resistant to accepting immigrants. But Japan retains a high standard of living, a highly skilled labor force, a stable society, relatively clean air and water, and areas of technological leadership and manufacturing skills. Moreover, its culture (both traditional and popular), its overseas development assistance, and its support of international institutions provide resources for soft power.

It is unlikely that Japan will become a global challenger to the United States, economically or militarily, as was predicted late in the last century. Roughly the size of California, Japan will never have the geographical or population scale of the United States. Its success in modernization and democracy and its popular culture provide Japan with some soft power, but ethnocentric attitudes and policies undercut it. Some leaders have started a movement to revise Article 9 of the constitution, which restricts Japan's forces to self-defense, and a few have spoken of nuclear armament. If the United States were to drop its alliance with Japan, it could produce the sense of insecurity that might lead Japan to decide it had to develop its own nuclear capacity, but even so it would be far from a peer competitor.

Alternatively, if Japan were to ally with China, the combined resources of the two countries would make a potent coalition. In 2006, China became Japan's largest trade partner, but an alliance seems unlikely because of territorial disputes in the East China Sea, and because the historical trauma of the 1930s has never completely healed. China and Japan have conflicting visions of Japan's proper place in the world. For example, China has opposed Japan's efforts to win a permanent seat on the UN Security Council. China would want to constrain Japan, but Japan would chafe at the restraints. In the highly unlikely prospect that the United States were to withdraw from the East Asian region, Japan might join a Chinese bandwagon. But given Japanese concerns about the rise of Chinese power, continued alliance with the United States is the more likely outcome. In terms of a traditional balance of power resources, Japan is more likely to seek American support to preserve its independence from China, and this enhances the American position. An allied East Asia is not a plausible path to an end of the American century.

In traditional realist terms, it is important that the two other entities in the world with high per capita income and advanced economies are both allied to the United States. That makes a large difference to the net position of American power. In addition, Europe and Japan provide the largest pools of resources for dealing with growing transnational problems. While their interests are not identical to those of the United States, the large amount of overlap of social and governmental networks among these societies are more likely to provide opportunities for cooperation for the joint creation of global public goods rather than an end to the American century.

Russia

In the 1950s, many Americans feared that the Soviet Union would surpass the United States as the world's leading power. The Soviet Union had the world's largest territory, third largest population, second largest economy, and produced more oil and gas than Saudi Arabia. It possessed nearly half the world's nuclear weapons, had more men under arms than the United States, and the highest number of people employed in research and development. Soviet propaganda actively fostered a myth of the inevitability of the triumph of communism, and Nikita Khrushchev famously boasted in 1959 that the Soviet Union would overtake the United States by 1970 or 1980. Instead, in 1986, Mikhail Gorbachev described the Soviet economy as "very disordered. We lag in all indices."[3] And in 1991, the USSR collapsed.

The collapse of the Soviet Union in 1991 left Russia with half the population and economy of the USSR. Moreover, the soft power of communist ideology, already eroded, had virtually disappeared. Russia retained a vast nuclear arsenal even larger than that of the United States, but its global power projection capabilities were greatly diminished. Regionally, however, it was able to use force effectively against its weak neighboring states – Georgia in 2008 and Ukraine in 2014.

In economic resources, Russia's \$2.5 trillion gross domestic product is one-seventh that of the United States, and its per capita income (in purchasing power parity) of \$18,000 is roughly a third that of the United States. Its economy is heavily dependent on energy. Oil and gas account for two-thirds of Russian exports, half of state revenues, and 20 percent of GDP. High-tech exports represent only 7 percent of its manufactured exports (compared to 28 percent for the United States). There is an inefficient allocation of resources across the economy, and private investment is not sustained because of a corrupt institutional and legal structure. Despite the attractiveness of traditional Russian culture and President Vladimir Putin's calls for an increase in Russian soft power, his bullying tactics toward his neighbors and his emphasis on Russian nationalism had the opposite effect of sowing mistrust. Few foreigners watch Russian films, and only one Russian university is ranked in the top global 100.

The likelihood of ethnic fragmentation, though still a threat in areas like the Caucuses, is less than in Soviet days. Non-Russians made up half of the former Soviet population; they are now 20 percent of the Russian Federation and occupy 30 percent of the territory. The political institutions for an effective market economy are largely missing, and robber baron state capitalism lacks the kind of effective regulation and rule of law that creates trust. The public health system is in disarray, mortality rates have increased, and birth rates are declining. The average Russian male dies in his early sixties, an extraordinary statistic for an advanced economy. Mid-range estimates by UN demographers suggest that Russia's population may decline from 145 million today to 121 million by mid-century.

Many futures are possible, but at this point Russia appears to be in decline – a "one crop economy" with corrupt institutions and insurmountable demographic and health problems. This decline should not be exaggerated, since Russia has talented human resources and some areas like the defense industry can produce sophisticated products. Some analysts believe that with reform and modernization, Russia will be able to surmount these problems, and former President Dmitry Medvedev, who worried that Russia would stagnate in a "middle income trap," laid out plans "for Russia to modernize its economy, wean itself from a humiliating dependence on natural resources and do away with Soviet-style attitudes that he said were hindering its effort to remain a world power."[4] But little has been implemented, and pervasive corruption has made modernization difficult. Under Vladimir Putin, Russia's post-imperial transformation has failed and it remains preoccupied with its place in the world and torn between its historical European and Slavophile identities.

Declining powers like the Austro-Hungarian and Ottoman Empires in 1914 can prove highly disruptive in the international system. Putin's Russia lacks a strategy for long-term recovery and reacts opportunistically (and sometimes successfully in the short run) to domestic insecurity, perceived external threats, and the weakness of neighbors. Russia thus becomes a revisionist spoiler of the status quo seeking to become a catalyst for other revisionist powers which chafe at American pre-eminence. But an ideology of anti-liberalism and Russian nationalism is a poor source of soft power. Rather than having a universal appeal beyond Russia's borders, it tends to be self-limiting by creating mistrust. Thus the prospects for Russian plans for a Eurasian Union to compete with the European Union are limited.

Whatever the outcome of Putin's revisionism, because of its residual nuclear strength, its oil and gas, its skills in cyber technology, its proximity to Europe, and the potential of alliance with China, Russia will have the resources to cause problems for the United States, and Putin's reliance on populist nationalism for domestic support provides an incentive. But Russia will not have the capacity to balance American power that it had during the Cold War, nor is its challenge likely to be the cause of the end of the American century.

What are the prospects for a Russia–China alliance being the cause? Traditional balance of power politics might predict such a response to American primacy in power resources. And there is historical precedent: in the 1950s, China and the Soviet Union were allied against the United States. After Nixon's opening to China in 1972, the triangle worked the other way, with the United States and China cooperating to limit what both saw as a threatening Soviet power. That alliance ended with the collapse of the Soviet Union. In 1992, Russia and China declared their relations a "constructive partnership," in 1996 a "strategic partnership," and in

July 2001 they signed a treaty of "friendship and cooperation." They have cooperated closely in the UN Security Council and taken similar positions on international control of the internet. The have used various diplomatic frameworks, such as the BRICS and the Shanghai Cooperation Organization, to coordinate positions, and Presidents Putin and Xi Jinping have struck up a good working relationship based on common domestic illiberalism and a desire to counter American ideology and diplomacy.

Despite the rhetoric, however, there are serious obstacles to an alliance between China and Russia that go a long way beyond tactical diplomatic coordination. As a rising power, China has more to gain than Russia from the status quo, including access to American trade and technology. Moreover, a residual historical mistrust persists between Russia and China. They compete for influence in Central Asia, and Russians are rankled by China's view of trade with Russia as exchanging manufactures for raw materials. The demographic situation in the Far East, where the population on the Russian side of the border is 6 million, and on the China side is up to 120 million, creates a degree of anxiety in Moscow. Russia's economic and military decline has increased its concern about the rise of Chinese power. In 2009, Russia announced a new military doctrine that explicitly reserved the right to first use of nuclear weapons (as the United States did to deter Soviet conventional superiority in Europe during the Cold War), and it continues to hold a large number of short-range tactical nuclear weapons. Many military observers believe the Russian doctrine is a response to Chinese conventional superiority in East Asia.

Russia still poses a potential threat to the United States, largely because it is the one country with enough missiles and nuclear warheads to destroy the United States, and its relative decline has made it more reluctant to renounce its nuclear status. Russia also possesses enormous scale, an educated population, skilled scientists and engineers, and vast natural resources. But it seems unlikely that Russia would again possess the resources to present the same sort of balance to American power that the Soviet Union presented during the four decades after World War II, or that its recovery would precipitate the end of the American century.

India

With a population of 1.2 billion people, India is four times larger than the United States, and likely to surpass China in population by 2025. Some Indians predict a tripolar world by mid-century: the United States, China, and India. But population alone is not an index of power unless those human resources are developed, and India has lagged seriously behind China in terms of literacy and economic growth rates.

For decades, India suffered from what some called the "Hindu rate of economic growth" of a little over 1 percent per capita. After independence in 1947, India followed an inward-looking planning system that focused on heavy industry. After market-oriented reforms in the early 1990s, the pattern changed and growth rates rose to over 7 percent. Higher projections of double digits failed to materialize, however, and before the 2014 elections, growth had slumped to 5 percent. After the election, a new prime minister, Narendra Modi, vowed to reverse the slump. India has an emerging middle class of several hundred million, and English is an official language spoken by some 50 to 100 million. Building on that base, Indian information industries are able to play a global role, and India has an active space program, which sent a satellite to Mars in 2014.

India has significant military power resources, with an estimated 90 to 100 nuclear weapons, intermediate range missiles, 1.3 million military personnel, and annual military expenditure of nearly $50 billion – or 3 percent of the world total. In terms of soft power, India has an established democracy, and a vibrant popular culture with transnational influence. India has an influential diaspora, and its motion picture industry, "Bollywood," is the largest in the world in terms of the number of films produced yearly, out-competing Hollywood in parts of Asia and the Middle East, and now Latin America.

At the same time, India remains very much an underdeveloped country, with hundreds of millions of illiterate citizens living in poverty. Around a third of India's 1.1 billion people live in conditions of acute poverty. India's GDP of $3.3 trillion is little over a third of China's $8 billion, and 20 percent that of the United States. India's per capita income of $2,900 (in purchasing power parity) is half of China's and a fifteenth of the United States. Even more striking, while 95 percent of the Chinese population is literate, the number for India is only 63 percent. Each year, India produces about twice as many engineers as America, but, according to *The Economist*, fewer than one-fifth of them "are employable by an IT services company, even with six months' training."[5] A symptom of this is the

40

poor performance of India in international comparisons of universities, with none ranked in the top 100. India's high-tech exports are only 5 percent of its total exports, compared to 30 percent for China.

India is unlikely to develop the power resources to become a global challenger to the United States in the first half of this century, but it has considerable assets that could be added to the scales of a Sino-Indian coalition. Trade between the two countries is growing rapidly, but the likelihood that such a coalition would become a serious anti-American alliance is small. Just as there is lingering suspicion in the Sino-Russian relationship, so there is a similar rivalry between India and China. While the two countries signed agreements in 1993 and 1996 that promised peaceful settlement of the border dispute that led them to war in 1962, the border became controversial again after Chinese actions in 2009. While Indian officials are often discreet in public about relations with China, their security concerns remain intense in private. Rather than becoming an ally, India is more likely to become part of the group of Asian nations that will tend to balance China. It has already begun to strengthen its diplomatic relations with Japan. It seems unlikely that a challenge from India will precipitate the end of the American century.

Brazil

Brazil is another significant member of the BRICS group, and the largest country in Latin America. It is the seventh largest economy in the world, though 95th in per capita income. After curbing inflation and instituting market reforms in the 1990s, Brazil grew at an impressive rate of 5 percent in the ensuing decade, though this slowed in recent years. With a territory nearly three times the size of India's, 90 percent of its 200 million people literate, a $2.5 trillion GDP equivalent to Russia's, and per capita income of $12,000 (three times that of India), Brazil has impressive economic power resources. In 2007, the discovery of massive offshore oil reserves promised to make Brazil a significant player in the energy arena. Its military is much smaller, and it has no nuclear weapons. On the other hand, it is the largest state on its continent, and has no real peer competitors among its neighbors. In soft power terms, its popular culture of carnival and football has transnational appeal, and it has adapted a foreign policy designed to project a positive image in Latin America and beyond.

Brazil faces a serious number of problems. Its infrastructure is inadequate, its legal system overburdened, it has a very high murder rate, and

serious corruption problems. It ranks 72nd out
of 175 countries on Transparency International's
corruption perceptions index (compared to 80th
for China, 94th for India and 127th for Russia).
In economic competitiveness, the World Economic
Forum ranks Brazil as 57th among 144 countries
(compared to 28th for China, 71st for India, and
53rd for Russia). Brazil spends less than the OECD
average on research and development; and South
Korea, with a population a quarter of Brazil's,
registers about 30 times more patents. Productivity
growth has been "almost stagnant since 2000;
today it is just over half the level achieved in
Mexico."[6] Although Brazil is the home of some successful transnational corporations, such as Embraer
and Vale, as one Brazilian manager put it, "we are
not going to have a Harvard or a Google here."[7]
Some Brazilian analysts believe that they will not
be able to raise their productivity rate unless they
increase their savings and invest more in education.

In terms of foreign policy objectives, Brazil has
resisted a number of requests from the United
States to alter its policy toward countries like Iran
and Venezuela. On the other hand, Brazil has not
made notable progress on its main policy objectives
of a permanent seat on the UN Security Council,
a world trade deal, and completion of a powerful

South American bloc. While the new Brazil will complicate American diplomacy compared to the past, it is unlikely that Brazil will try to become a peer competitor to the United States. That role will be left to China, and while Brazil finds diplomatic coordination with China to be useful, there are sharp limits to the relationship. Again, it is difficult to see the growth of Brazil overtaking the United States and helping to precipitate the end of the American century.

The only country potentially capable of such a role is China. Among the BRICS, China is by far the giant, with an economy equal to the other countries combined. It has the largest army, the largest military budget, the highest rate of economic growth, and the most internet users. China lags behind Russia and Brazil in income per capita, but this may change if China maintains its high growth rates. At any figure above 7 percent per year, the Chinese economy will double in a decade. China recovered quickly from the 2008 economic crisis, and, as we saw earlier, many analysts expect the total size of the Chinese economy to surpass that of the United States in the near future. Beyond that, one Nobel laureate economist has projected that by 2040, China will produce 40 percent of global GDP (and the United States, Europe, and Japan only 21 per cent).[8] As the *Financial Times* columnist Gideon Rachman observed, "Americans can be forgiven if they greet talk of a new challenge from China as just another case of the boy who cried wolf. But a frequently overlooked fact about that fable is that the boy was eventually proved right. The wolf did arrive – and China is the wolf."[9] We turn to China in the next chapter.

4

The Rise of China

Many analysts view China as the most likely contender to balance American power, surpass it, and end the American century. The historian Niall Ferguson has said "the 21st century will belong to China." One recent book is even entitled *When China Rules the World: The End of the Western World and the Birth of a New Global Order.*"[1] Already in the 1990s, polls showed half the American public thought China would pose the biggest challenge to US world power status in the twenty-first century.[2]

While most projections of Chinese power are based on the rapid growth rate of its GDP, China also has other significant power resources. Its territory is equal to that of the United States and its population is four times greater. It has the world's largest army, more than 250 nuclear weapons, and modern capabilities in space and cyber space (including the world's largest number of internet users.) In soft power resources, China still lacks cultural industries able to compete with Hollywood or Bollywood; its universities are not top ranked; and it lacks the many nongovernmental organizations that generate much of America's soft power. However, it has always had an attractive traditional culture, and it has created hundreds of Confucius Institutes around the world to promote it.

Already in the 1990s, I wrote that the rapid rise of China might cause the type of conflict described by Thucydides when he attributed the Peloponnesian War to the rise in the power of Athens and the fear it created in Sparta.[3] The political scientist John Mearsheimer flatly asserts that China cannot rise peacefully.[4] Historical analogies are also drawn to World War I, when Germany had surpassed Britain in industrial power and the Kaiser was pursuing an adventurous, globally oriented foreign policy that was bound to bring about a clash with other great powers.

In contrast, China still lags far behind the United States in all three dimensions of power, and has focused its policies primarily on its region and on its economic development. While its "market Leninist" economic model provides soft power in some authoritarian countries, it has the opposite effect in many democracies.[5] Nonetheless, the rise of China recalls Thucydides' other warning that belief in the inevitability of conflict can become one of its main causes.[6] Each side, believing it will end up at war with the other, makes reasonable military preparations which then are read by the other side as confirmation of its worst fears. In this regard, a possible source of optimism is Jonathan Fenby's judgment that China "will not have the economic, political and human resources to dominate the world, even if it wished to do so."[7]

Economic power

The "rise of China" is a misnomer; recovery is more accurate. China was the world's largest economy until it was overtaken by Europe and America in the past two centuries as a result of the industrial revolution. After Deng Xiaoping's market reforms in the early 1980s, China's high annual growth rates of 8 to 10 percent led to a remarkable tripling of its GDP in the last two decades of the twentieth century, and many believe it will soon regain its place as the world's largest economy.

Nonetheless, China has a long way to go to equal

the power resources of the United States, and it still faces many obstacles to its development. Currently, the American economy is about twice the size of China's at official exchange rates, but, as mentioned in Chapter 1, China will soon pass the United States if measured at purchasing power parity (PPP). All such comparisons and projections are somewhat arbitrary because they depend on the questions one wants to answer. PPP is an estimate that economists make to compare welfare in different societies, but it is also sensitive to population size. Thus India, the tenth largest economy measured at the dollar/rupee exchange rate, comes out as the world's third largest in terms of PPP. On the other hand, comparisons in terms of current exchange rates, although they may fluctuate depending on currency values, are often more accurate in estimating power resources. The value of a given salary in terms of being able to buy a haircut or a house is best compared by using PPP. On the other hand, the cost of imported oil or parts for an advanced aircraft engine is better judged at the exchange rates that must be used to pay for them.

Even if overall Chinese GDP passes that of the United States (by whatever measure), the two economies will be equivalent in size, but not equal in composition and sophistication. China still has a vast underdeveloped countryside and faces a number of challenges, including rapid urbanization. Per capita income provides a better measure of the sophistication of an economy, and even measured in PPP, China's per capita income is only 20 percent of the American level and it will take decades to catch up (if ever).

Of course, total size is an important aspect of economic power. Having a large attractive market and being the largest trading partner for a large number of countries is an important source of leverage, which China wields frequently. But that is not the same as equality. For example, although China surpassed Germany in 2009 as the world's largest trading nation in terms of volume, the Chinese are concerned that their country "has yet to develop into a truly strong trading country," because trade in services is lackluster, many exports have low added value, and China lacks "top notch brands compared with world trade powerhouses like the United States and Germany" (19 of the top 25 global brands are American).[8] Of transnational corporations, 46 percent of the top 500 are owned by Americans.[9] In other words, Chinese trade is larger but relatively less sophisticated than that of the United States or Germany.

Another illustration comes in the monetary area.

China has studied the power (including financial sanctions) that the United States derives from the role of the dollar in the world. China has tried to increase its financial power by encouraging the use of the yuan for trade finance, and it now represents 9 percent of the global total. But the dollar still accounts for 81 percent. The role of the yuan will increase, but it is unlikely to displace the dollar until China lets international markets set exchange rates, and develops deep and sophisticated domestic capital markets and an accompanying legal structure that engenders trust. As *The Economist* notes, "size and sophistication do not always go together .... In the 2020s China will probably be the world's biggest economy, but not its most advanced. America's sophistication is reflected in the depth of its financial markets." China's are only one-eighth as big and foreigners are permitted to own only a tiny fraction of these.[10]

Technology is yet another example of differences in sophistication. China has important technological achievements, but it also has relied heavily on a strategy of copying foreign technologies more than domestic innovation. In the words of the Chinese journal *South Reviews*, "China boasts the title of the largest factory powerhouse in the world [and] China-based patents are growing fast and exceeding those of developed countries. But most patents obtained in China are less important in the entire industrial chain . . . . In short, China remains weak in science and technological innovation."[11] Chinese often complain that they produce iPhone jobs, but not Steve Jobs. The trade volume shows up in Chinese statistics, but the value added shows up in the US figures.

Looking ahead, at some point China's growth will slow, as all economies do once they develop. Some economists think China's growth will slow to 5 percent as it downsizes wasteful political investment in the inefficient state-owned sector, and it may have trouble maintaining that level as demographic problems set in after 2020.[12] But even at lower rates China could continue to grow faster than much of the world. However, linear projections of growth trends can be misleading, because countries tend to pick the low hanging fruit as they benefit from imported technologies and cheap labor in the early stages of economic take-off, and growth rates generally slow as economies reach the per capita levels of income (in PPP) that China is now approaching. This so-called "middle income trap" is not an iron law (as Japan and South Korea proved), but a regularity that many countries encounter if they fail to innovate and change their growth model. President

Xi Jinping is well aware of the problem, and China is trying to implement market reforms to avoid it.

The Chinese economy faces serious obstacles of transition from inefficient state-owned enterprises, growing inequality, environmental degradation, massive internal migration, an inadequate social safety net, corruption, and an inadequate rule of law. The north and east of the country have out-paced the south and west. Only 10 of 31 provinces have per capita income above the national average, and underdeveloped provinces include those with higher proportions of minorities, such as Tibet and Xinjiang. Moreover, China will begin to face demographic problems from the delayed effects of the one child per couple policy it enforced in the twentieth century.[13] Newcomers to China's labor force started to decline in 2011, and China's labor force will peak in 2016. China is aging very rapidly: by 2030 it will have more elderly dependents than children. Chinese express concern that their country is "getting old before getting rich."

Reducing saving and increasing domestic con-sumption as China plans is an obvious but not easy answer, because an aging population may keep household savings high, and high corporate savings reflect special interests and limited competi-tion in some sectors. And although China holds the world's largest foreign currency reserves of nearly $4 trillion, it will have difficulty in increasing its financial leverage until it has an open bond market where interest rates are set by the market and not the government. Nor does China's massive holding of dollars give it much direct bargaining power with the United States, because in an interdependent relationship power depends on asymmetries in the interdependence. China holds dollars it receives from its sales to America, but the United States keeps its market open to Chinese products and that creates growth, jobs, and stability back in China. Despite irritations and temptations, China has not dumped its dollars on world financial markets. If it were to do so, it might bring America to its knees, but at the cost of bringing itself to its ankles.

China's authoritarian political system has thus far shown an impressive power conversion capability in relation to specific targets – for example, building impressive new cities and high-speed rail projects. Whether China can maintain this capability over the longer term is a mystery both to outsiders and to Chinese leaders. Unlike India, which was born with a democratic constitution, China has not yet found a way to solve the problem of demands for political participation (if not democracy) that tend to accompany rising per capita income. The

ideology of communism is long gone, and the legitimacy of the ruling party depends upon economic
growth and ethnic Han nationalism. Will economic
change bring political change when per capita GDP
approaches $10,000 (PPP), as occurred in neighbor-
ing South Korea and Taiwan? There are now more
billionaires in "communist" China than any country other than the United States, and the rich are not
just getting richer, but "doing so at the expense of
the poorest people in the land."[14] Whether China
is able to develop a formula that can manage an
expanding urban middle class, regional inequality,
and resentment among ethnic minorities remains to
be seen. The basic point is that no one, including
Chinese leaders, knows how China's political future
will evolve and how that will affect its economic
growth.

Cyber politics presents another complication.
With 600 million users, China has the largest
internet population, as well as a highly developed
system of governmental controls and filters. Not
only are many internet users intensely nationalistic,
but minority liberal views are filtered out and dis-
sent is punished. Companies self-censor and follow
government orders. Nonetheless, some leakage
of information is inevitable. Coping with greatly
increasing flows of information at a time when

restrictions can hinder economic growth presents a sharp dilemma for Chinese leaders. Though the Communist Party elite is unlikely to lose control of the population, a China that cannot control flows of migration, environmental effects on the global climate, and internal conflict would pose a different set of serious problems. Politics sometimes has a way of confounding economic projections.

Military power

As long as China's economy grows, it is likely that its military expenditure will increase. China spends about 2 percent of GDP on the military (half the US level), but GDP is growing rapidly. China's official 2014 budget of $132 billion was about a quarter of the American budget, but Chinese statistics on military expenditure do not include many items that are listed in the American defense budget. The International Institute of Strategic Studies adds another $20–30 billion to the official number. After a period of low investment, from 1989 to 2009 China's official military budget increased by double digits every year, and in 2013 it rose 12 percent. Once a large technologically unsophisticated force focused on land defense against the Soviet Union, the People's Liberation Army today has evolved into a more modern force focused on countering intervention by the United States in the East Asia region.

At the same time, China's 11 percent of global military expenditure is far less than the American 39 percent. At current growth rates, China's military expenditure may be half that of the United States by 2020, and it may come close to parity in mid-century, but in accumulated stocks of modern military equipment, the United States retains at least a 10:1 advantage over China without even counting American allies.[15] China has not developed significant capabilities for global force projection, and while it has increased its ability to complicate American naval operations off its coast, it is only just beginning the complex process of developing a blue water navy with carrier battle groups. As China becomes increasingly dependent on Middle Eastern oil, its navy will be relevant to smooth passage through the Strait of Malacca in Southeast Asia, but the American navy will remain crucial to the Strait of Hormuz in the Persian Gulf.

With one refurbished Ukrainian carrier (and two more at various stages of planning), China is still decades behind America's 10 carrier battle groups with long experience in global maneuvers. China is developing two different prototypes of fifth-generation stealth fighter aircraft, but again without the global reach of the Americans. At the global level, China has a limited number of intercontinental ballistic missiles and has been making impressive efforts to develop asymmetrical conflict capabilities in space and cyberspace, but it is still not the equal of the United States in these domains. And in the conventional arena, it lacks the alliances, overseas bases, long-range logistics, and the expeditionary experience of American forces. While the United States has some 240,000 troops based in dozens of foreign countries, China has a few thousand engaged primarily in UN peacekeeping missions.

The fact that China will not soon be a peer in global power projection should not detract from the fact that China's investments in fighters, submarines, cruise missiles, and intermediate range ballistic missiles have already increased the costs of any American intervention in the seas near China's coasts. Global military reach should not be conflated with regional military effectiveness. If current trends continue and the United States wishes to continue to reassure its allies in the region, it will need to reduce its force vulnerability in the face of China's strategy of area denial. This will require costly investments such as stealthy unmanned aerial vehicles that can operate from carrier flight decks, submarines with greater land attack capacity, local ballistic missile defenses, a more resilient system of smaller satellites, and offensive cyber capabilities.[16]

Soft Power

In 2007, then President Hu Jintao told the Chinese Communist Party that China needed to increase its soft power. For a rising power like China, whose growing economic and military might frightens its neighbors into counterbalancing coalitions, a smart strategy includes soft power to make China look less frightening and the balancing coalitions less effective.

The soft power of a country rests primarily on three resources: its culture (in places where it is attractive to others), its political values (when it lives up to them at home and abroad), and its foreign policies (when they are seen as legitimate and having moral authority.) But combining hard and soft power resources into a smart strategy is not always easy. For example, establishing a Confucius Institute in Manila to teach Chinese culture may help produce soft power, but it is less likely to succeed in a context where China is bullying the

Philippines over possession of disputed islands in the South China Sea. As China becomes more assertive in its territorial claims toward its neighbors, it makes it more difficult to achieve the objective of increasing its soft power.

Moreover, much of America's soft power is produced by civil society – everything from universities and foundations to Hollywood and pop culture – not from the government. Sometimes the United States is able to preserve a degree of soft power because of its critical and uncensored civil society even when government actions – like the invasion of Iraq – are otherwise undermining soft power. But in a smart power strategy, hard and soft reinforce each other.

In his book *China Goes Global*, David Shambaugh details how China has spent billions of dollars on a charm offensive to increase its soft power. Chinese aid programs to Africa and Latin America are not limited by the institutional or human rights concerns that constrain Western aid. The Chinese style emphasizes high-profile gestures. But for all its efforts, China has had a limited return on its investment. Polls show that opinions of China's influence are positive in much of Africa and Latin America, but predominantly negative in the major powers of the United States, Europe, India, and Japan.

The Rise of China

The 2008 Beijing Olympics was a soft power success, but shortly afterwards, China's domestic crackdown on human rights activists undercut its soft power gains. The 2009 Shanghai Expo was also a great success, but it was followed by the jailing of Nobel Peace Laureate Liu Xiaobo and television screens around the world were dominated by scenes of an empty chair at the Oslo ceremonies. Marketing experts call this "stepping on your own message." China's subsequent punishment of Norway by restricting imports of salmon did not help the situation.

China makes the mistake of thinking that government is the main instrument of soft power. In today's world, information is not scarce but attention is, and attention depends on credibility. Government propaganda is rarely credible. The best propaganda is not propaganda. For all the efforts to turn Xinhua and China Central Television into competitors for CNN and the BBC, there is little international audience for brittle propaganda. As *The Economist* noted about China, the party has not bought into "Nye's view that soft power springs largely from individuals, the private sector, and civil society. So the government has taken to promoting ancient cultural icons whom it thinks might have global appeal."[17]

The development of soft power need not be a zero sum game. All countries can gain from finding each other attractive. But for China to succeed, it will need to restrain its claims upon its neighbors, and this is difficult in a period of rising nationalism. With regard to more distant countries in Europe or North America, it will need to be self-critical and unleash the full talents of its civil society, but this is difficult in a period when the Communist Party is pursuing tighter controls. While China's economic success, its economic aid programs, and its hundreds of Confucius Institutes teaching culture can all enhance China's soft power, it will remain limited so long as the domestic constraints of rising nationalism and party control remain strong.

China's strategy and American responses

The current generation of Chinese leaders, realizing that rapid economic growth is the key to domestic political stability, has focused on economic development and what they call a "harmonious" international environment. But times change, power often creates hubris, and appetites sometimes grow with eating. Martin Jacques argues that "rising powers in time invariably use their newfound economic strength for wider political, cultural and military ends. That is what being a hegemonic power involves, and China will surely become one."[18] Chinese leaders have created a myth that China has never invaded its neighbors or behaved "hegemonically," but, as Foreign Minister Yang Jiechi famously told an ASEAN meeting in 2010, "China is a big country and other countries are small countries, and that is just a fact."

Traditionally, China saw itself as the center or "middle kingdom" of a tributary system of states in East Asia, and some analysts believe it will seek to recreate this order.[19] Others, like John Ikenberry, argue that the current international order has the openness, economic integration, and capacity to absorb China rather than be replaced by a Chinese-led order.[20] Thus far, Chinese leaders have taken only minor steps toward a major global role, whether hegemonic or as a "responsible stakeholder."

Some analysts have argued that China aims "in the near term to replace the United States as the dominant power in East Asia and in the long term to challenge America's position as the dominant power in the world." Others say China seeks to divide the Pacific and drive the American presence beyond the chain of islands off its coast (that includes Japan).[21] Many experts disagree over whether these simplifications are an accurate assessment of China's intentions. China has benefited greatly from the existing international institutional order, but it also wants to make some changes, and even Chinese cannot know the views of future generations.[22]

More important, it is doubtful that China will have the military capability to make overly ambitious dreams possible in the next several decades. Costs matter. It is easier to indulge one's wish list when a menu has no prices on it. Chinese leaders will have to contend with the reactions of other countries as well as the constraints created by their own objectives of economic growth and the need for external markets and resources. Too aggressive a Chinese military posture could produce a countervailing coalition among its neighbors in the region that would weaken both its hard and soft power.

The fact that China is not likely to become a peer competitor to the United States on a global basis does not mean that it could not challenge the United States in Asia, but, as mentioned earlier, the rise of Chinese power in Asia is contested by India and Japan (as well as smaller neighbors such as Vietnam), and that provides a major power advantage to the United States.[23] The US–Japan alliance, which the Clinton-Hashimoto declaration of 1996 reaffirmed as the basis for stability in post-Cold War East Asia, is an important impediment to Chinese ambitions, as is the improvement in US–India relations, and Japan–India relations. This means that in the great power politics of the region, China cannot easily expel the Americans. From that position of strength, the United States, Japan, India, Australia, and others can work to provide incentives for China to play a responsible role, while hedging against the possibility of aggressive behavior as China's power grows.

American responses

Looking ahead, pessimists predict an impending clash as China grows stronger and seeks to expel the United States from the Western Pacific. Some argue that this can be forestalled by the acceptance of spheres of influence in which the United States restricts its activities primarily to the Eastern Pacific. But such a response to China's rise would destroy American credibility and lead regional states into bandwagoning rather than balancing China. Such a policy could indeed represent the beginning of the end of the American century. Instead, a continued US presence can reinforce the natural balancing reactions of regional states and help to shape the environment in a way that encourages responsible Chinese behavior.

An appropriate policy response to the rise of China must balance realism and integration. When the Clinton Administration first considered how to respond to the rise of China in the 1990s, some critics urged a policy of containment before China became too strong. Such advice was rejected for two reasons. First, it would have been impossible to forge an anti-China alliance, since most countries in the region wanted (and still want) good relations with both the United States and China. Even more important, such a policy would have unnecessarily guaranteed future enmity with China. Instead, the United States chose a policy that could be called "integrate and insure." China was welcomed into the World Trade Organization, but the US–Japan security treaty was revived to insure against China becoming a bully. If a rising China throws its weight around, it drives neighbors to seek to balance its power. In that sense, only China can contain China.

This is a key point in assessing the relative power of the United States and China. As Yan Xuetong wrote about how China could defeat America, "to shape a friendly international environment for its rise, Beijing needs to develop more high-quality diplomatic and military relationships than Washington. No leading power is able to have friendly relations with every country in the world, thus the core of competition between China and the United States will be to see who has more high-quality friends."[24] At this point, the United States is better placed to benefit from such networks and alliances. Washington has some 60 treaty allies; China has few. In political alignments, *The Economist* estimates that of the 150 largest countries in the world, nearly 100 lean toward the United States, while 21 lean against.[25]

In 2011, the United States announced a strategy of rebalancing toward Asia, the fastest growing part of the world economy. Some Chinese see the Obama Administration policy of "rebalancing" toward Asia as a form of containment, but whereas under the Cold War doctrine the United States had virtually no trade or social contact with the Soviet Union, it has massive trade with China, and some 230,000 Chinese students attend American universities. Shaping the environment for Chinese decisions is a more accurate description than containment for American strategy.

The Rise of China

Some analysts see China as a revisionist state eager to overthrow the established international order as its strength increases. But China is not a full-fledged revisionist state like Nazi Germany or the Soviet Union in the last century. While it has joined in the creation of a BRICS development bank, and promotes regional organizations that suit its needs, China has benefited greatly from, and is not eager to destroy, existing international institutions such as the UN, the International Monetary Fund, the World Bank, and the World Trade Organization – as well as many others. Out of self-interest, it has played a role in stabilization of monetary crises in the past two decades.[26] Europe, Japan, and India are significant powers that help shape an international environment that encourages responsible behavior, and China cares about its reputation. At the same time, however, as China's economic power increases, it will be better placed to resist such pressures.

In addition, technological and social changes are adding a number of important transnational issues to the global agenda, such as climate change, pandemics, terrorism, organized crime, and cyber crime. These issues represent not a transition of power among states, but a diffusion of power away from all governments. Coping with these global threats will require increased intergovernmental cooperation that includes China, Europe, and the United States, and others.

China aspires to play a larger role in East Asia and the United States has Asian allies to whose defense it is committed. Miscalculations are always possible, but conflict is far from inevitable. The legitimacy of the Chinese government depends on a high rate of economic growth and the top leaders realize that China will need many decades before it approaches the sophistication of the American economy. Where Germany was pressing hard on Britain's heels (and passed it in industrial strength), as we have seen, the United States remains decades ahead of China in overall military, economic, and soft power resources at the global level. Moreover, China cannot afford a policy like that of the Kaiser's Germany. Too adventuresome a policy risks its gains and stability at home and abroad.

In other words, the United States has more time to manage its relations with a rising power than Britain did a century ago, and China has incentives for restraint. Too much fear can be self-fulfilling. Whether the United States and China will manage their relationship well is another question. Human error and miscalculation are always possible. But, with the right choices, a regional war is not inevitable, and the rise of China globally is a long process that is still far from signifying the end of the American century.

5

Absolute Decline: Is America Like Rome?

Are we Rome? After Cullen Murphy asked that question in the title of a popular book, he concluded "maybe."[1] Rome did not succumb to the rise of another empire. As we saw earlier, it suffered an absolute decline in its society, economy, and institutions that left it unable to protect itself from hordes of invading barbarian tribes. Some analysts argue that the costs of exercising power externally weakens domestic economies and contributes to absolute decline because of "imperial overstretch."[2] Thus far, the American facts do not fit that theory very well because defense and foreign affairs expenditures have declined as a share of GDP over the past several decades.

Nonetheless, the United States could decline in terms of relative power not because of "imperial overstretch," but for domestic reasons. Rome rotted from within when people lost confidence in their culture and institutions, elites battled for control, corruption increased, and the economy failed to grow.[3] Could the United States lose its ability to influence world events because of domestic battles over culture, collapse of institutions, and economic stagnation? If the economy fails, the United States will lose hard as well as soft power. And even if the United States continues to hold impressive military, economic, and soft power resources, it could lack the capacity to transform those resources into effective influence.

Society and culture

Culture is never static and critics often lament the ways of the current generation. For example, where some people point to growing materialism or changing sexual mores or the coarseness of popular culture as proof of absolute decline, others see striking changes in gender and race relations as progress. While the United States has many social problems, these do not seem to be getting worse in any linear manner. Some are even decreasing, such as crime, divorce rates, and teenage pregnancy. While there are culture wars over issues like same sex marriage and abortion, polls show an overall increase in tolerance. Civil society is robust, and polls show that weekly church attendance at 37 per cent is only slightly lower than a decade ago. The media has a natural tendency to emphasize bad news (because it sells), and reaction to national trends is a mediated phenomenon. If everyone "knows" from the media that things are a mess in Washington and they have no direct experience at that level, they tell pollsters the conventional wisdom about the national condition. The resulting polls are not convincing evidence of decline. Past culture battles over slavery, prohibition, McCarthyism, and civil rights were more serious than any of today's issues. People often attribute a golden glow to the past and that makes it easy to assert decay.

Culture wars could adversely affect American power if citizens become so distracted or divided by domestic battles over social and cultural issues that the United States loses the capacity to act collectively in foreign policy. That appeared to be a problem in the 1970s in the aftermath of deep divisions over Vietnam. More recently, one might cite President Obama's damaging postponement of a trip to Asia owing to a government shutdown over budget issues in 2013, which repeated a similar postponement for similar reasons by President Clinton in 1995.

Deterioration of American social conditions could also reduce soft power. Although America has made progress on some social issues, the United States lags behind other rich countries on infant mortality, life expectancy, children in poverty, incarceration, and homicides. Such comparisons can be costly for American soft power, but the United States is not alone in many of the cultural changes that cause controversy in developed countries. Respect for authority and some standards of behavior have declined since 1960 throughout the Western world, but there is little indication that American levels are systematically lower than others. Some behaviors, such as charitable giving and community service, are generally higher. On the other hand, a recent index of "livability" ranks the US 16th out of 132 countries.[4]

Immigration is a sensitive social issue in many developed countries, but America is one of the few that may avoid demographic decline and keep its share of world population, largely as a result of immigration. Current fears over the effect of immigration on national values and on a coherent sense of American identity are nothing new. The nineteenth-century "Know Nothing" Party was built upon opposition to immigrants, particularly the Irish. A century later, the country elected an Irish Catholic president. The United States remains a nation of immigrants with a creed of opportunity for newcomers. During the twentieth century, America recorded its highest percentage of foreign-born residents in 1910: 14.7 percent of the population. A century later, about 40 million people or nearly 13 percent of Americans today are foreign-born citizens.

Despite being a nation of immigrants, a recent Pew poll shows 36 percent of Americans want legal immigration to be limited. Both the numbers and origins of the new immigrants have caused concerns about immigration's effects on American culture. Data from the 2010 census showed a soaring Hispanic population driven largely by waves of new immigrants, legal and illegal. At 16 percent of the total population, Hispanics have replaced Blacks as the nation's largest minority. Critics fear they will not assimilate, but most of the evidence suggests that the latest immigrants are assimilating at least as quickly as their predecessors. While too rapid a rate of immigration can cause social problems, over the long term, immigration tends to strengthen the power of the United States.

Most developed countries will experience

a shortage of people as the century progresses, whereas the US Census Bureau projects that between 2010 and 2050, the American population will grow by 42 percent to 439 million. Today the United States is the world's third most populous country. Fifty years from now it will still likely remain one of the top three or four. Not only is this relevant to economic power, but, given the fact that nearly all developed countries are aging and face a burden of providing for the older generation, immigration could help reduce the sharpness of that policy problem. As for direct effects, studies show that as the number of immigrant college graduates grows, so does the increase in patents per capita. A quarter of high-tech start-ups have an immigrant founder, and 40 per cent of Fortune 500 companies were founded by immigrants or their children.[5]

Immigration also benefits America's soft power. The fact that people want to come to the United States enhances American appeal, and the upward mobility of immigrants is attractive to people in other countries. America is a magnet, and many people can envisage themselves as Americans. Moreover, connections between immigrants and their families and friends back home help to convey accurate and positive information about the United States. Rather than diluting hard and soft power, immigration enhances both. As Lee Kwan Yew, an astute observer of both the United States and China, once told me, the United States recreates itself by attracting the best and brightest from the rest of the world and melding them into a diverse culture of creativity. China has a larger population to recruit from domestically, but, in his view, its Sino-centric culture makes it less creative than the United States.

The Economy

The cultural and social problems discussed thus far do not indicate an impending domestic decline that is likely to weaken America's external power, but a long-term slump in the level of productivity and the capacity for sustained economic growth could do so. While macroeconomic forecasts are always imprecise, it appears that the United States is experiencing slower growth in the decade following the 2008 financial crisis than the type of no growth that plagued Japan in the decade after its speculative bubble burst in the early 1990s. The International Monetary Fund expects American economic growth to average about 2–3 percent in coming years. This is lower than the potential, but it is not stagnation. Contrary to popular expectations of bleak economic prospects, at 2 percent growth, national income will double in 35 years.

In the 1980s, many observers believed that American dominance had been lost, and this contributed to the mood of decline mentioned above. The annual rate of increase of labor productivity, which averaged 2.7 percent in the two decades after World War II, had slipped to 1.4 percent in the 1980s. Japan and Germany were believed to be overtaking America and this undercut American hard and soft power. The United States seemed to have lost its competitive edge. Today, however, even after the financial crisis and ensuing recession, the World Economic Forum ranked the United States 3rd out of 154 countries in global economic competitiveness, with no major economies ahead of it. In comparison, China ranked 28th.[6] Niall Ferguson points out that this is a drop from first place in 2008–9, but it is unclear how much this reflects the recession or the excessive legislation, regulation, and institutional decline that he cites. At the same time, the American economy leads in many new sectors that will be critical in this century, such as information technology, biotechnology, and nanotechnology.

Will productivity growth support American power well into this century, or will there be an absolute decline? Optimists cite the US lead in the production and use of information technologies. In the 1990s, a noticeable reduction in the cost of computing power enhanced American productivity, but it was not the only source. The United States has seen significant agricultural innovation, and openness to globalization also plays a role.

Energy is another source of optimism because of the shale revolution that started in the United States. While the technologies of horizontal drilling and hydraulic fracturing are not new, their pioneering application to shale rock is largely a product of American entrepreneurship since the early 2000s. At the turn of the century, many experts thought that the production of oil in the world economy had peaked. The United States was projected as being increasingly weakened by dependence on energy imports and was building terminals to import high priced liquefied natural gas. Instead, it is now converting terminals to export its low cost LNG, and the North American continent is expected to approach self-sufficiency in energy in the 2020s. The US Department of Energy estimates that when recoverable resources of shale energy are combined with other oil and gas resources, they could last for two centuries.[7]

The shale revolution has a number of economic

implications. Some benefits are the obvious product of market forces. Shale energy production boosts the economy and produces jobs. Reducing imports helps the balance of payments. New revenues ease government budgets. Cheaper energy makes industry more competitive internationally, particularly energy-intensive industries like petrochemicals, aluminum, steel, and others. There are also psychological effects on markets. For some time, increasing dependence on energy imports was often cited as evidence of decline. Not only does the shale revolution change that dependence, but it illustrates the combination of entrepreneurship, property rights, and capital markets that represents the underlying strength of the American economy.

In overall research and development, the United States was the world leader, with $465 billion in 2014, or a 31 percent share of the global total (compared to China at 17.5 percent and Japan at 10.3 percent.) The United States spent 2.8 percent of its GDP on research and development, slightly less than the roughly 3.5 percent each for Japan and Korea.[8] In 2014, American inventors registered about 133,000 patents in the United States, or 48 percent of the total.[9] A number of reports have expressed concern about matters such as corporate tax rates, human capital, and the growth of overseas patents. Others argue that Americans are more innovative at using and commercializing technologies because it has an entrepreneurial culture, the most mature venture capital industry, a tradition of close relations between universities and industry, and an open immigration policy.

Other concerns about the future of the American economy include the low rate of personal savings, the current account deficit (which means that Americans are becoming more indebted to foreigners), and the rise in government debt. Personal savings are difficult to calculate and subject to serious measurement errors, but the trend was clearly down from 9.7 percent of personal incomes in the 1970s to near zero in 2001, recovering to about 4 percent after the financial crisis of 2008–9.[10] How much it matters is difficult to determine. In addition to personal savings, the national savings rate includes government and corporate savings. Japan kept up a high personal savings rate, but its economy stagnated. When corrected for the fact that capital goods are cheaper in the United States, American real investment compares favorably with other OECD countries. The danger is that in a severe recession, foreigners might withdraw their investments rapidly and add to instability in the economy, but contrary to such dire predictions, the dollar remained a safe haven after the 2008 crisis.

After the financial crisis, a major source of concern became the level of government debt. In the words of a British historian, "this is how empires decline. It begins with a debt explosion." Ferguson went on to say that "the idea that the US is a 'safe haven' is nonsense. Its government debt is a safe haven the way Pearl Harbor was in 1941 ... The gross federal debt in public hands will exceed 100 percent of GDP in just two years' time."[11] Others are less alarmist, pointing out that the federal deficit is now a manageable 3 percent of GDP, that debt as a percentage of GDP is declining modestly, and that Japan has a government debt twice the size of that of the United States. The longer-term forecast, however, is more concerning unless policy is altered. According to the Congressional Budget Office, the deficit could equal 6.5 percent of GDP by 2039.

Education is another concern, since it is key to economic success in an information age. At first glance, the United States does well. According to the Department of Education in 2013, 88 percent of adults graduate from high school and 32 percent graduate from college. American university graduation rates are higher than most countries, and the United States spends nearly twice as much on higher education as a percentage of GDP than do any of France, Germany, Britain, or Japan. The American higher education system is rated the best in the world, and American universities have widened their lead in academic reputation over competitors in Britain, Continental Europe, and Japan over the past few decades. A study by Shanghai Jiao Tong University places 17 of the top 20 universities in the US (and none in China).[12] Americans win more Nobel prizes than do citizens of any other country, and publish more scientific papers in peer-reviewed journals. These accomplishments enhance both economic power and soft power.

However, while American education is strong at the top, it is less impressive at lower levels. Higher education and the top slice of the secondary system set the global standard, but too many primary and secondary schools in less affluent districts lag badly behind. This could mean that the quality of the labor force will not keep up to the rising standards needed in an information-based economy. A National Assessment of Educational Progress in 2013 found only 42 percent of fourth-graders were at or above the proficient level in math, and only 35 percent scored at that level in reading, though there was a slight improvement over the decade.[13] A 2013 report by the Organization for Economic

Cooperation and Development comparing adult skills in 20 advanced countries found that 36 million Americans have low skills and young American workers ranked last in numeracy and technological proficiency. It is not clear that students are performing worse than in the past, but America's educational advantage is being eroded because more countries are doing better than in the past.[14] Among the 30 richest countries, only New Zealand, Spain, Turkey, and Mexico now have lower high school completion rates.[15] American students do not seem to be improving their knowledge and skills enough to keep pace with an advancing economy.

The changing shape of the nation's income distribution also poses a potential problem for the American economy. From 1947 to 1968, the Census Bureau shows that family income inequality decreased, but after 1968 it increased. The American Gini coefficient of .42 is relatively high by international standards and "has risen steadily over the past several decades."[16] The richest 10 percent of the population take a larger slice of the economic pie than they did in 1913. The share of personal income going to the top 1 percent has risen by 10 percentage points over the past generation and the share of the bottom 90 percent has fallen by a similar amount. Technological change and shifts in labor demand away from less-educated workers are perhaps the most important factors in explaining why the income gap between the richest and poorest have widened sharply in most advanced countries over the past quarter century. For our purposes, the question is whether inequality affects hard and soft power. Economists disagree about whether it slows growth, and thus far inequality has not changed class mobility for most people in the United States. We do know that it affects the health and education opportunities of the less skilled part of the workforce, and this is bad not only for labor productivity but also for equality of opportunity.[17] It may also lead to further political entrenchment of a political elite as well as broad political reactions that could curb the productivity of the economy.

The soft power of the American economy is often debated. Many people admire the success the American economy has had over the long term, but criticize it as a model. Government plays a lighter role in the US economy, spending about 40 per cent of GDP (at all levels), while Europe is nearer one-half. There is underinvestment in public goods such as infrastructure. Competitive market forces are stronger, social safety nets weaker. Unions are weaker and labor markets more flexible and less regulated. American health care has been both costly and unequal. Cultural attitudes, bankruptcy laws, and financial structures more strongly favor entrepreneurship. Regulations are more trans-parent, and shareholders have more influence on company managers. While foreigners extol some of these virtues, others object to the price of inequal-ity, insecurity, and macroeconomic instability that accompanies this greater reliance on market forces. Despite these problems and uncertainties, it is inaccurate to describe the American economy as in absolute decline, and it seems likely that it will continue to produce hard external power for the country.

Political institutions

Greater uncertainty surrounds the question of American institutions. Many observers believe that gridlock in the American political system will pre-vent it from translating its power resources into power outcomes. Francis Fukuyama argues that "American society is not in decline because the overall situation of the economy is relatively strong, but that the political system has been subject to con-siderable decay."[18] While partisan gridlock today has been rising, the question is how much worse the situation is than in the past. Sarah Binder says the "distance between the parties ideologically has all but returned to heights not seen since the end of the 19th century." While the second Congress under President Obama tied with the second Congress under President Clinton as the most gridlocked, the intervening 111th Congress managed to pass a major fiscal stimulus, health care reform, financial regulatory system, an arms control treaty, and revision of military policy on homosexuality. Binder speculates that it "may well be correct that our political system will weather this rough patch with little harm done. Even so we are left in the meantime with a national legislature plagued by low legislative capacity."[19] A Pew poll finds that while ideological consistency has doubled over the past two decades, from 10 to 21 percent, most Americans do not have uniformly conservative or liberal views, and want their representatives to meet halfway. Nonetheless, the parties have become more consistently ideological since the 1970s.[20]

Power conversion – translating power resources into effective influence – is not a new problem for the United States. The Constitution is based on an eighteenth-century liberal view that power is best controlled by fragmentation and countervailing checks and balances rather than centralization.

Absolute Decline: Is America Like Rome?

American government was designed to be inefficient so that it presented less threat to liberty. In foreign policy, the Constitution was written in a way that invites the President and Congress to struggle for control. Strong economic and ethnic pressure groups struggle for their self-interested definitions of the national interest, and press Congress to legislate the tactics of foreign policy and codes of conduct with sanctions for other countries. As Henry Kissinger once pointed out, "what is presented by foreign critics as America's quest for domination is very frequently a response to domestic pressure groups."[21]

Polls show a decline of public confidence in institutions. In 1964, three-quarters of the American public said they trusted the federal government to do the right thing most of the time. Today only a fifth of the public express trust at this high standard. The numbers have varied somewhat over time, rising in the patriotic climate after September 11, 2001 before gradually declining again (though the numbers for state and local government have been slightly better).[22] Government is not alone. Over the past few decades, public confidence has dropped in half for many major institutions: 61 to 30 percent for universities; 55 to 13 percent for major companies; 73 to 33 percent for medicine; and 29 to 11 percent for journalism. Over the past

88

decade, confidence rose in educational institutions and the military, but fell for Wall Street and major companies.[23]

A long Jeffersonian tradition says Americans should not worry too much about the level of confidence in government. Moreover, when asked not about day-to-day government but about the underlying national and constitutional setting, the public is very positive. If you ask Americans what is the best place to live, 82 percent say the United States. If asked whether they like their democratic system of government, 90 percent say yes. Few people feel the system is rotten and must be overthrown.[24]

Some aspects of the current mood are probably cyclical, while others represent discontent with current bickering and deadlock in the political process. Compared with the recent past, party politics has become more polarized, but nasty politics goes all the way back to the founding fathers. Part of the problem of assessment is that faith in government became abnormally high among the generation that survived the depression and won World War II. In that case, over the long term, the anomaly was overconfidence in government in the 1950s and early 1960s, not low levels thereafter. Moreover, much of the evidence for loss of trust in government comes from polling data, and while there has been a downward trend to answers to the same questions over time, the significance of this decline is still uncertain. After all, the sharpest decline occurred four decades ago in the late 1960s and early 1970s, not in the most recent decade.

As yet, the behavioral results have been limited. For example, the Internal Revenue Service sees little increase in cheating on taxes, despite the decline in confidence in the polls.[25] The World Bank gives the United States a high score (90th percentile) on "control of corruption."[26] Voluntary mail return of census forms increased to 67 percent in 2000, and remained there in 2010, reversing a 30-year decline since 1970.[27] Voting rates declined from 62 percent to 50 percent over the latter half of the twentieth century, but the decline stopped in 2000, and returned to 58 per cent in 2012. Behavior does not seem to have changed as dramatically as have responses to poll questions. The causes of the expressed loss of confidence in institutions may be rooted in deeper trends in attitudes toward individualism and less deference to authority that are characteristic of all postmodern societies.

How serious are these changes in social capital for the effectiveness of American institutions? Robert Putnam notes that community bonds have not weakened steadily over the last century. On the contrary, American history carefully examined is a story of ups *and* downs in civic engagement, not just downs – a story of collapse and renewal.[28] Three-quarters of Americans feel connected to their communities and say the quality of life there is excellent or good. Nearly half of adults take part in a civic group or activity. Moreover, the American system is federal and more decentralized than most. Partisan gridlock in the national capital is often accompanied by political cooperation and innovation at the state and urban government levels. As *The Economist* commented, "America's political system was designed to make legislation at the federal level difficult, not easy. Its founders believed that a country the size of America is best governed locally, not nationally . . . So the basic system works; but that is no excuse for ignoring areas where it could be reformed."[29] Whether the American political system can reform itself and cope with the problems described above remains to be seen, but it is not as broken as implied by critics who draw analogies to the domestic decline of Rome or characterize the country as suffering paralysis. As the conservative author David Frum notes, over the past two decades, the United States has seen a swift decline in crime, auto fatalities, emissions that cause acid rain, abortions, alcohol and tobacco consumption, while leading an internet revolution.[30] On the other hand, the question remains as to whether the political institutions are up to the needs of effective power conversion in the twenty-first century.

Conclusions

As we saw earlier, ancient Rome had an economy without productivity, a society riven by internecine warfare, and rampant corruption and decay in political institutions that made Rome incapable of defending itself. The facts above make it hard to draw a sustainable analogy between the United States and Rome. American culture has cleavages, but they remain manageable and less dangerous than at times in the past. Social problems abound, with some getting worse and some better. The society remains open to the outside world and better able than most to renew itself by immigration. The American economy is growing more slowly than in the past, but it remains innovative at using and commercializing technologies because of its entrepreneurial culture, the most mature venture capital industry, and a tradition of close relations between industry and the world's top ranking universities. It leads the world in research and development, and is at the forefront of new cyber, nano, bio, and energy technologies.

Real problems exist in terms of inequality and educating the workforce of the future. The largest questions are about political institutions. Political gridlock was incorporated into the American system from the start, but it has been increasing in Washington in recent years. Even if they are not worse than in the past, the important question is whether the institutions will be able to cope with the problems of the future. At the same time, the federal system also ensures diversity and the potential for innovation in states and cities. And the lesser role of government means that much of the innovation in America occurs outside government and outside Washington. Moreover, despite the increased partisan bickering, several serious problems, ranging from deficits to energy to health care costs, have improved rather than deteriorated in recent years. America has many problems and they raise many questions, but they are not creating an absolute decline that gives us a clear answer about when the American century will end.

6

Power Shifts and Global Complexity

There are two great power shifts occurring in this century; power transition among states from West to East, and power diffusion from governments to non-state actors as a result of the global information revolution.[1] I argued above that the first shift – power transition among states – will probably not end American centrality to the global balance of power in the next 30 years.

It is less clear whether this shift will destroy the institutions that Amitav Acharya, cited earlier, calls "the American world order." His metaphor of a multiplex theater with multiple narratives and regional dialogues assumes an architecture but includes little detail about how it will be provided and maintained. Will China step in to provide the public goods that hegemonic stability theorists search for? Certainly China has benefited greatly from liberal institutions like the World Trade Organization and the International Monetary Fund, but China's record is far from perfect. Like the United States in the interwar period of the last century, China enjoys the temptation of free-riding as long as someone else is driving the bus. Nor are we likely to see global public goods provided by other emerging powers.

Greater complexity

At the same time, the diffusion of power from governments to non-state actors, both West and East, is putting a number of transnational issues like financial stability, climate change, terrorism, and pandemics on the global agenda at the same time that it tends to weaken the ability of all governments to respond. Since no one state can deal successfully with these transnational issues acting alone, even a superpower will have to work with others.

After the collapse of Cold War bipolarity, power in this global information age became distributed in a pattern that resembles a complex three-dimensional chess game. On the top chessboard, military power is largely unipolar and the United States is likely to retain primacy for quite some time. But on the

certain trends are visible now and can be projected to continue, "other things being equal" (which they sometimes will not be.) For example, demographic trends tend to be more predictable than political events, and it is likely that the United States will grow in population, while Europe, Russia, Japan, and China will shrink. Equally interesting, however, is that the population of the African continent will more than likely double. Although this does not mean that an African country will challenge the pre-eminence of the United States, it does suggest that certain areas of the world will present more complex problems, particularly when a rising population is combined with rapid urbanization and inadequate educational institutions and social security systems.

One can also project economic trends, though, as we have seen, one should be less confident about the predictions they yield. For example, the United States entered the twenty-first century with a 23 percent share of world GDP and, even before the Great Recession, this was gradually declining not because of American failure, but because of the rapid growth in the rest of the world, including not only China but many other emerging economies. Contrary to some assertions that the American share of world output remains unchanged, it has actually slipped.[6] Projecting forward to 2018, the International Monetary Fund estimates that the United States will then represent about 17.7 percent of the world economy.[7] The diminishing American share is not unique. From 2001 to 2010, the West's share of the world economy shrank by 10.33 percentage points, more than the combined loss of the previous 40 years. While part of this was a product of the recession, it also represented faster growth in other parts of the world economy. And since these include America's closest allies, it represents a loss for American networks.

Even though this growth in emerging markets is unlikely to create a single challenger that will overtake the United States, the "rise of the rest" creates a more complex world to be faced. In contrast, in the 1960s, the United States and Europe together represented two-thirds of the world economy, with Japan adding a further 10 percent.[8] Moreover, the number of countries in the world has more than trebled over that period. There are more demands for seats at the table, and that means that negotiating trade standards, aviation agreements, telecommunications regulations, environmental agreements, and others becomes more complex to manage. New organizations like the Group of 20 can help, but they leave out most states and even 20 is an unwieldy number. One could call these trends "relative decline," but that description confuses the situation with the rise of identifiable challengers, and it seems more useful to refer simply to the rise of the rest.

Some observers see this entropy spelling chaos in the global economy, and argue that although the United States will be hurt, it will be better placed to cope with entropy than other nations.[9] But this exaggerates the problem of entropy, and underestimates the remaining American role. For example, in the economic crisis conditions of 2008, agreement among the G20 leaders helped to restrain protectionism, but the US Federal Reserve's informal network of agreements to swap dollars among central banks proved essential. The financial crisis was damaging to American hard and soft power, but the US remained crucial to its management.[10]

The problem of leadership in such a world is how to get everyone into the act and still get action. And the American role in galvanizing institutions and organizing informal networks remains crucial to answering that puzzle. As we saw earlier, there has often been self-serving exaggeration about the American provision of public goods in the past, but a case can be made for Goliath. As Michael Mandelbaum describes the American role, other countries will criticize it, but "they will miss it when it is gone."[11]

More important, it is not yet gone. Even in issues where its pre-eminence in resources has diminished, American leadership often remains critical to global collective action. Take trade and non-proliferation of nuclear weapons as two examples of important economic and security issues where American dominance is not what it once was.

In trade, the United States was by far the largest trading nation when the GATT (General Agreement on Tariffs and Trade) was created in 1947, and the United States deliberately accepted trade discrimination by Europe and Japan as part of its Cold War strategy. After those countries recovered, they joined the United States in a club of like-minded nations within the GATT.[12] In the 1990s, as other states' shares of global trade increased, the United States supported the expansion of GATT into the World Trade Organization and the club model became obsolete. The United States supported Chinese accession to the World Trade Organization and China passed the United States as the world's largest trading nation. While global rounds of trade negotiations became more difficult to accomplish and various free trade agreements proliferated, the rules of the World Trade Organization continued to provide a general structure wherein the norm of most favored nation status and reciprocity created a framework in which particular club deals could be generalized to a larger number of countries. Moreover, new entrants like China found it in their interests to observe even adverse judgments of the World Trade Organization dispute settlement process.

Similarly with the non-proliferation regime: in the 1940s, when the United States had a nuclear monopoly, it proposed the Baruch plan for UN control, which the Soviet Union rejected in order to pursue its own nuclear weapons program. In the 1950s, the United States used the Atoms for Peace program, coupled with inspections by a new International Atomic Energy Agency, to try to separate the peaceful from the weapons purposes of nuclear technology as it spread. In the 1960s, the five states with nuclear weapons negotiated the non-proliferation treaty, which promised peaceful assistance to states that accepted a legal status of non-weapons states. In the 1970s, after India's explosion of a nuclear device and the further spread of technology for enrichment and reprocessing of fissile materials, the United States and like-minded states created a Nuclear Suppliers Group, which agreed "to exercise restraint" in the export of sensitive technologies, as well as an International National Nuclear Fuel Cycle Evaluation, which called into question the optimistic projections about the use of plutonium fuels. While none of these institutional adaptations was perfect, and problems persist with North Korea and Iran today, the net effect of the normative structure and American leadership was to slow the growth in the number of nuclear weapons states from the 25 expected in the 1960s to the 9 that exist today.[13] In 2003, the US launched the Proliferation Security Initiative, a loosely structured grouping of countries that shares information and coordinates efforts to stop trafficking in nuclear proliferation related materials.

Similar questions arise today about the governance of the internet and cyber activities. In its early days, the internet was largely American, but today China has twice as many users as the United States. Where once only Roman alphabet characters were used on the internet, now there are top-level domain names in Chinese, Arabic, and Cyrillic scripts, with more alphabets expected. And in 2014, the United States announced that it would relax the Commerce Department's supervision of the internet's "address book," the International Corporation for Assigned Names and Numbers (ICANN). Some observers worried that this would open the way for authoritarian states to try to exert control and censor the addresses of opponents.

Such fears seem exaggerated both on technical grounds and in their underlying premises. Not only would such censorship be difficult, but there are self-interested grounds for states to avoid such fragmentation of the internet. In addition, the descriptions in the decline in American power in the cyber issue are overstated. Not only does the United States remain the second largest user of the internet, but it is the home of eight of the ten largest global information companies.[14] Moreover, when one looks at the composition of important non-state voluntary communities (like the Internet Engineering Task Force), one sees a disproportionate number of Americans participating because of their expertise. The loosening of US government influence over ICANN could be seen as a strategy for strengthening the institution and reinforcing the American multistakeholder philosophy rather than as a sign of defeat.[15] Some cyber stability now exists, but the fact that cyber insecurity creates inherent risks for both the United States and its opponents provides a basis for possible agreements.[16] In short, projections based on theories of hegemonic decline can be misleading about the realities of American leadership in international institutions and networks. Even with diminishing power resources, American leadership remains essential in creating public goods.

The information revolution and power diffusion

The growth in the number and wealth of states is not the only source of increased complexity in this century. The problem for all states in today's global information age is that more things are happening outside the control of even the most powerful governments, or what I have called the diffusion of power. Moises Naim refers to the rise of "micro powers" and says "the decoupling of the capacity to use power effectively from the control of a large Weberian bureaucracy is changing the world."[17] In an information-based world, power diffusion is a more difficult problem to manage than power transition. Conventional wisdom has always held that the government with the largest military prevails, but in an information age it may be the state (or non-states) with the best story that wins. Soft power becomes a more important part of the mix.

Governments have always worried about the flow and control of information, and the current period is not the first to be strongly affected by dramatic changes in information technology. Gutenberg's printing press was important to the origins of the Protestant Reformation and the turmoil that followed in Europe. Today, however, a much larger part of the population both within and among countries has access to the power that comes from information. It is not surprising to find turmoil, for example, in parts of the Middle East. As the UN's Arab Human Development Report indicated, a region that lagged in literacy, science, non-energy trade, and information was ripe for disruption by the information revolution, and the religious and political disruptions may last for a generation. A number of analysts have compared the region today to Germany at the time of the Thirty Years' War in the seventeenth century.

The current information revolution is based on rapid technological advances that have dramatically decreased the cost of creating, finding, and transmitting information. Following "Moore's Law," computing power doubled every 18 months for 30 years, and by the beginning of the twenty-first century it cost one-thousandth of what it did in the early 1970s. If the price of automobiles had fallen as rapidly as the price of semiconductors, a car would cost about $15–20. The key characteristic of this information revolution is not merely the *speed* of communications, but the enormous reduction in the *cost* of transmitting information that reduces the barriers to entry.

In the middle of the twentieth century, people feared that the computers and communications of the current information revolution would bring to life George Orwell's *1984*, with central planning and surveillance powers at the top of a pyramid of control. It is true that cheap computing and data storage make government surveillance easier. Authoritarian governments like China, Saudi Arabia, and others use such techniques to try to control their citizens, but cheap computing and big data also empower private companies to try to steer the preferences of their customers. And organized criminal groups can create insecurity by preying upon these transactions.

At the same time, as computing power has decreased in cost and computers that once filled a room have shrunk to the size of smart phones and other portable devices that fit in your pocket, their decentralizing effects have outweighed their centralizing effects. Power over information is much more widely distributed today than it was even a few decades ago. Flash mobs and demonstrations around the world challenge governments' efforts to shut down access to the internet, text messaging, and television.

Power Shifts and Global Complexity

What this means is that world politics will not be the sole province of governments. Individuals and private organizations, ranging from WikiLeaks to corporations to NGOs to terrorists to spontaneous societal movements, are all empowered to play direct roles in world politics. The spread of information means that power will be more widely distributed and informal networks will undercut the monopoly of traditional bureaucracy. The speed of internet time means all governments have less control over their agendas. Political leaders enjoy fewer degrees of freedom before they must respond to events, and then must communicate not only with other governments but with civil societies as well – witness the difficulties the Obama Administration had trying to fine tune its responses to the events of the Arab revolutions that were misleadingly called " the Arab Spring."

In principle, as it reduces costs and barriers of entry into markets, the information revolution could reduce the power of large states and enhance the power of small states and non-state actors. But it would be a mistake to "over-learn" the lessons of the Egyptian and other revolutions. Politics and power are more complex than such technological determinism implies. After its initial embarrassment by Twitter in 2009, the Iranian government was able to suppress the green movement in 2010. And while the "great fire-wall of China," is far from perfect, the government has managed thus far to cope with information flows among the 600 million internet users in the country. Yet social media have had a subtle impact on the availability of information in China.

Some aspects of the information revolution help the small; but some help the already large and powerful. Size still matters. While a hacker and a government can both create information and exploit the internet, it matters for many purposes that large governments can deploy tens of thousands of trained people and have vast computing power to crack codes or intrude into other organizations. Even though it is now cheap to disseminate existing information, the collection and production of new information often requires major investment, and in many competitive situations, *new* information matters most. Intelligence is a good example. Cyber security is another example, where the elaborate Stuxnet worm that disabled Iranian nuclear centrifuges is reported to have been a product of governments.

On the other hand, greater capability and connectedness also creates greater vulnerability. The information revolution is increasing the diffusion of power in this century. Governments and large states still have larger resources, but the stage on which they play is more crowded with information-empowered private actors – including transnational companies, terrorists, mobs, criminals, or individuals. We are only just beginning to comprehend the effects of the information revolution on power in this century. The one clear point is that the growth in complexity of the international system makes governmental control more difficult. It is an oversimplification to see contemporary world politics as an "age of entropy" or "the end of power," but control will be more difficult for all actors. And in such circumstances, as Moises Naim argues, the government vacuum throws up "terrible simplifiers" – demagogic populists of the left and right who further deepen paralysis without offering real solutions.[18] Or as David Brooks has put it, "political leaders are not at the forefront of history; real power is in the swarm."[19] This may not spell the end of the American century, but it does signify a more complex context that makes wielding power more difficult. In addition to a lot more actors – both state and non-state – the agenda of international politics is becoming increasingly complex. Not only do traditional issues of security and the economy remain important, but the number of transnational issues has increased and many of these are not susceptible to traditional hard power instruments. For example, military power is of little help on climate change, pandemics, or the governance of the internet.

Under the influence of the information revolution and globalization, world politics is changing in a way that means the United States cannot achieve many of its international goals acting alone. For example, international financial stability is vital to the prosperity of Americans, but the United States needs the cooperation of others to ensure it. Global climate change will affect the quality of life, but Americans cannot manage the problem alone. And in a world where borders are becoming more porous to everything from drugs to infectious diseases to terrorism, nations must use soft power to develop networks and build institutions to address shared threats and challenges.

The United States will remain the largest country in the international system, and the case for the largest country providing leadership in organizing the production of global collective goods remains strong. In some areas of military and economic goods, American leadership can provide a large part of the answer. For example, the American navy is crucial in policing the law of the seas, and as we saw in the 2008–9 financial crisis, the confidence that comes from having a lender of last resort was provided by the Federal Reserve.

But on the new transnational issues, while American leadership will be important, as we showed above, success will require the cooperation of others. In this sense, power becomes a positive sum game. If the American century is to continue, it will not be enough to think in terms of American power *over* others. One must also think in terms of power *to* accomplish joint goals which involves power *with* others. On many transnational issues, empowering others can help the United States to accomplish its own goals. In this world, networks and connectedness become an important source of relevant power. The American century will continue in the sense of the centrality of the United States to the balance of power and American leadership in the production of public goods, but it will look different from how it did in the latter half of the last century.

7

Conclusions

Any effort to assess American power in the coming decades should recall how many earlier efforts have been wide of the mark. It is chastening to remember how wildly exaggerated were American estimates of Soviet power in the 1970s and of Japanese power in the 1980s. Today, some analysts confidently predict China will replace the United States as the world's leading state, while others equally confidently argue that "the United States is only at the beginning of its power. The twenty-first century will be the American century."[1] But unforeseen events can confound such projections. There is a range of possible futures, not just one, and the alternatives involve accidents, miscalculations, and idiosyncratic human choices.

Conclusions

Net assessment and the balance of power

American power relative to China will depend on the uncertainties of future political change in both countries. If China does not encounter adverse uncertainties, its size and high rate of economic growth will almost certainly increase its relative strength, and bring it closer to the United States in power resources over the next few decades. These relative gains do not necessarily mean that China will surpass the United States as the most powerful country. As we saw earlier, even if China suffers no major domestic political setback, many current projections based on GDP growth are simple linear extrapolations of current growth rates that are likely to slow down in the future. Moreover, economic projections are one dimensional and ignore US military and soft power advantages, as well as China's geopolitical disadvantages in the internal Asian balance of power, compared to America's likely favorable relations with Europe, Japan, India, and others. Imagine how different the American situation would look if, instead of oceans and two friendly neighbors, it bordered a score of states, some (like Japan or India) both skeptical and powerful.

My guess is that among the range of possible

futures, ones in which a new challenger such as Europe, Russia, India, Brazil, or China surpasses the United States and precipitates the end of the American centrality to the global balance of power are not impossible, but not very likely. Moreover, as the British strategist Lawrence Freedman notes, unlike "the dominant great powers of the past: American power is based on alliances rather than colonies."[2] Alliances and informal networks are assets; colonies are liabilities.

On the question of absolute rather than relative American decline, we saw that the United States faces serious problems in areas like debt, secondary education, income inequality, and political grid-lock, but one should note that they are only part of the picture. On the favorable side of the ledger are the trends in demography, technology, and energy, as well as abiding advantages such as geography and an open entrepreneurial culture. American problems are real, and failure to address them will weaken the country's ability to cope with growing global complexity, but it is worth distinguishing situations where there are no solutions from those which could in principle be solved. If one looks for scenarios which could precipitate decline, among the negative futures are ones in which the United States becomes too fearful and overreacts to terrorist attacks by closing inwards and thus cutting itself off from the strength its obtains from openness. Alternatively, it could overreact by becoming overcommitted and waste blood and treasure as it did in Vietnam and Iraq.

As an overall assessment, describing the twenty-first century as one of American decline is likely to be inaccurate and misleading. The language of "decline" is confusing. For example, from 1945 to 1970, American policies deliberately created relative decline, which Richard Nixon and Henry Kissinger then interpreted as a long-term trend. But by the end of the century, the United States was the world's only superpower. More important, talk of "decline" can lead to dangerous policy choices if it encourages countries like Russia to engage in adventurous policies, China to be more assertive with its neighbors, or the United States to over-react out of fear. America has many problems, but it is not in absolute decline, and even in relative terms it is likely to remain more powerful than any single state in the coming several decades. The real problem for the United States is not that it will be overtaken by China or another contender, but that it will be faced with a rise in the power resources of many others – both states and non-state actors. This diffusion of power will make the United States relatively less able to control others. Entropy may prove a greater challenge than China. Moreover, the world will face an increasing number of new transnational issues which will require power *with* others as much as power *over* others. In a world of growing complexity, the longstanding American inefficiency in power conversion may become a critical problem.

Strategy choices

Even if the United States continues to possess more military, economic, and soft power resources than any other country, it does not follow that it will choose to convert those resources into effective power behavior on the global scene. As we saw earlier, in the period between the two world wars, it chose not to do so. Some see this happening again. In the aftermath of a decade of wars in Iraq and Afghanistan, a 2013 poll found that 52 percent of Americans believed that "the US should mind its own business internationally and let other countries get along the best they can on their own." For the first time since Pew began asking in 1964, more than half of respondents said they agreed with that statement, which has historically ranged between about 20 and 40 percent. The share who said they disagreed with that statement was only 38 percent.

Some commentators immediately pronounced the return of isolationism in American foreign policy, but the word has become more a political cudgel than a term of analysis. As we saw earlier, American isolationism in the nineteenth century did not mean noninterference in the internal affairs of neighbors, but was more an attitude toward distant Europe, where the balance of global power was centered. The true isolationism of the 1930s was enshrined in various laws designed to prevent another intervention in Europe.

A better way to understand the current mood is to see it as part of a longstanding swing of a foreign policy pendulum between what Stephen Sestanovich has called "maximalist" policies and "retrenchment" policies.[3] Retrenchment is not isolationism, but an adjustment of strategic goals and means. Presidents who followed policies of retrenchment since the beginning of the American century have included Eisenhower, Nixon, Ford, Carter, the first Bush, and Obama. But while Nixon believed the United States to be in decline, others, like Eisenhower, did not. All of them were strong internationalists when compared to the true isolationists of the 1930s, but this did not protect them

118

from critics. For example, from the late 1930s to the late 1960s, the widely read columnists Joseph and Stewart Alsop were warning that weak and irresolute US leaders would open the door to our adversaries. "The Alsops' suspicion of Eisenhower was especially sharp," including a missile gap that turned out to be totally spurious.[4] Thus, when contemporary critics charge that "the Obama administration appears to be *intentionally* pursuing a policy of American decline," or that "retrenchment looks like weakness because it is weakness," the criticism tells us more about partisan politics than it does about whether the American century will end before 2041.[5]

Historians can make a credible case that periods of maximalist overcommitment have done more damage to America's power conversion capability than periods of retrenchment. A political reaction to Wilson's global idealism produced the intense isolationism that delayed America's response to Hitler; Kennedy and Johnson's escalation of the war in Vietnam produced an inward-oriented decade in the 1970s; and Bush's invasion of Iraq helped to create the poll numbers cited above. As Fareed Zakaria points out, when neo-conservatives extoll the "pervasive forward involvement" of the Roosevelt–Truman administration, their selective history leaves out the failures in the Soviet Union, China, and Korea that leaning forward was meant to deter but which happened anyway.[6]

Lurking behind the political polemics, however, is a serious set of policy debates and strategic choices that Americans must confront during a period of retrenchment. Among them, how much should the United States spend on defense and foreign policy? Some believers in imperial overstretch argue that the United States has no choice but to cut back on foreign and defense policy, but this is not the case. As a portion of GDP, the United States is spending less than half of what it did at the peak of the Cold War years when the American century was being consolidated. The problem arises when one looks at budgetary rather than macroeconomic constraints. The problem is not guns vs. butter, but guns vs. butter vs. taxes. Unless the budget is expanded by a willingness to raise taxes, defense and foreign affairs expenditure are locked in a zero sum trade-off, with important investments such as domestic repair of education, infrastructure, and spending on research and development. This can hurt both defense and domestic reform.

Another real debate is over intervention. How and in what way should the United States become involved in the internal affairs of other countries?

Conclusions

Obama has said that America should use military force, unilaterally if necessary, when its security or that of its allies is threatened. When this is not the case, but if conscience urges the country to react to situations such as a dictator killing a large number of his citizens, the United States should not act alone and should only use force if there is a good prospect of success. These are reasonable principles, but what are the thresholds for trading off values against practical realities? The problem is not new – John Quincy Adams wrestled with domestic demands for intervention in foreign wars of independence nearly two centuries ago. That is when he made his famous statement that America "goes not abroad in search of monsters to destroy" lest she "involve herself beyond power of extrication, in all wars of interest and intrigue, of individual avarice, envy, and ambition, which assume the colors and usurp the standard of freedom."

But what if forbearance in a civil war like Syria's allows a terrorist group to establish a safe haven such as the Taliban did in Afghanistan two decades ago or the Islamic State of Iraq and the Levant is trying to do? Some type of intervention may be necessary, but the United States should stay out of the business of invasion and occupation. In an age of nationalism and socially mobilized populations, foreign occupation is bound to breed resentment. Eisenhower wisely reached that conclusion in the 1950s, but what takes its place? Using force, but with limits, is an answer, but, particularly in the Middle East where revolutions may last another generation, smart application of force will be essential. Seen in a longer perspective, a Kennan-like policy of containment may have more promise than efforts to occupy and control.

Another debate is over how to build and bolster institutions, create networks, and establish policies for dealing with the new transnational issues discussed earlier. Leadership by the largest country is important for the production of global public goods. When the United States does less, others do less as well. Unfortunately, domestic political gridlock often blocks such leadership. For example, the US Senate has failed to ratify the Law of the Seas Treaty despite its being in the national interest and the fact that the United States needs it to bolster its diplomatic position in the South China Sea. Similarly, Congress failed to fulfill an American commitment to support the reallocation of International Monetary Fund quotas from Europe to emerging market countries, even though it would cost the United States almost nothing. And in terms of leading on responses to climate change, there is strong domestic resistance to putting a price on carbon emissions. Similarly, there is domestic resistance to international trade agreements. Such attitudes weaken the ability of the United States to take the lead in dealing with global public goods, and that in turn can weaken the legitimacy and soft power that are critical to the continuation of the American century.

Finally, the duration of the American century depends upon a broad set of alliances and will increasingly do so in the new context of world politics. How does the United States maintain the credibility of those alliances if other countries perceive the country as turning inward? At the same time, how does the United States prevent its balancing toward Asia from weakening its commitments in other regions like Europe and the Middle East? And in Asia, where cooperation as well as competition is essential in the strategy toward China, it will be important to avoid overmilitarizing the policy.

Military force will remain an important component of American power. Providing security to allies is an important source of influence, and limited interventions are often crucial. But force is a blunt instrument, and it is a mistake to equate leadership with unilateral military action. Those who point to the role of an American troop presence to the

Conclusions

economic and political success of Europe, Japan, and South Korea, for example, forget that the troops were welcome because of a clear and present external threat and even then it took more than three decades for democracy to emerge in Korea.

An American strategy that holds the military balance in Europe or East Asia has been important to the American century, but trying to occupy and control the internal politics of nationalistic populations in the Middle East revolutions can be a recipe for shortening it. And military force is not much help on transnational issues like the internet, climate change, or financial stability. If it wishes to prolong the American century, the United States must shape the international environment and create incentives for others through trade, finance, culture, and institutions, and forming networks and institutions for action. New types of networks and multistakeholder institutions will play a role. As former World Bank president Robert Zoellick has argued, "there are opportunities today to adapt the world to America's benefit that do not involve US military force."[7] More can be done with trade initiatives with Europe and Asia as well as a reduction of barriers to the integration of North America. While East Asia has been a region of economic dynamism, in the coming decades the demographic and energy situation will be more promising in North America. Even in East Asia, the United States needs to launch economic and ecological initiatives if it wishes to pursue an effective strategy for maintaining the American century. Ad hoc reactions to events are not enough. A period of retrenchment needs a smart power strategy.

* * *

In conclusion, the American century is not over, if by that we mean the extraordinary period of American pre-eminence in military, economic, and soft power resources that have made the United States central to the workings of the global balance of power, and to the provision of global public goods. Contrary to those who proclaim this the Chinese century, we have not entered a post-American world. But the continuation of the American century will not look like it did in the twentieth century. The American share of the world economy will be less than it was in the middle of the last century, and the complexity represented by the rise of other countries as well as the increased role of non-state actors will make it more difficult for anyone to wield influence and organize action. Analysts should stop using clichés about unipolarity and multipolarity. They will have to live with both in different issues at the same time.

Conclusions

And they should stop talking and worrying about poorly specified concepts of decline that mix many different types of behavior and lead to mistaken policy conclusions.

Leadership is not the same as domination. America will have to listen in order to get others to enlist in what former Secretary of State Hillary Clinton called a multipartner world. It is important to remember that there have always been degrees of leadership and degrees of influence during the American century. The United States never had complete control. As we saw in Chapter 1, even when the United States had preponderant resources, it often failed to get what it wanted. And those who argue that the complexity and turmoil of today's entropic world is much worse than the past should remember a year like 1956 when the United States was unable to prevent Soviet repression of a revolt in Hungary, French loss of Vietnam, or the Suez invasion by our allies Britain, France, and Israel. One should be wary of viewing the past through rose-tinted glasses. To borrow a comedian's line, "hegemony ain't what it used to be, but then it never was."

Now, with slightly less preponderance and a much more complex world, the United States will need to make smart strategic choices both at home and abroad if it wishes to maintain its position. The American century is likely to continue for a number of decades at the very least, but it will look very different from how it did when Henry Luce first articulated it.

Further Reading

There is no shortage of literature for readers who want to explore these questions further. With regard to Chapter 1, my book, *Presidential Leadership and the Creation of the American Era* (Princeton: Princeton University Press, 2013), looks at the choices made by crucial leaders in the past century. The second volume of Thomas G. Paterson, et al., *American Foreign Relations* (Stamford, CT: Cengage Learning, 2014) provides a standard history of the period. Walter Russell Meade offers an interesting interpretation in *Special Providence: American Foreign Policy and How It Changed the World* (New York: Knopf, 2001). For a classic radical view, see William A. Williams, *The Tragedy of American Diplomacy* (New York: Norton, 1972). Ernest May, *American Imperialism* (New York: Atheneum, 1968) paints a wonderful portrait of the United States during its brief period of formal imperialism at the turn of the twentieth century, and his *The World War and American Isolation, 1914–1917* (Chicago: Quadrangle, 1959) is

Further Reading

an excellent account of how the United States chose to enter that war. Robert Dallek, *Franklin D. Roosevelt and American Foreign Policy, 1932–1945* (Oxford: Oxford University Press, 1995) describes American entry into World War II, and the postwar period is well recounted in Walter Isaacson and Evan Thomas, *The Wise Men: Six Friends and the World They Made* (New York: Simon and Schuster, 1986.) Regarding the nature of the resulting postwar American order, see G. John Ikenberry, *Liberal Leviathan: The Origins, Crisis and Transformation of the American World Order* (Princeton: Princeton University Press, 2011). For a skeptical response, see Amitav Acharya, *The End of American World Order* (Cambridge: Polity, 2014).

On Chapter 2 and theories of hegemony and decline, Paul Kennedy's *The Rise and Fall of the Great Powers: Economic Change and Military Conflict Among the Great Powers* (New York: Random House, 1987) has become a classic account. Robert Gilpin, *War and Change in World Politics* (Cambridge: Cambridge University Press, 1981) gives a traditional realist account of hegemony, and Robert O. Keohane presents a liberal institutionalist alternative account in *After Hegemony: Cooperation and Discord in the World Political Economy* (Princeton: Princeton University Press, 1984). Regarding century-long cycles, see George Modelski, *Long Cycles in World Politics* (Seattle: University of Washington Press, 1987) for a mainstream effort, and Immanuel Wallerstein, *The Politics of the World Economy* (New York: Cambridge University Press, 1984) for a neo-Marxist version. Regarding the decline of British hegemony,

Further Reading

Corelli Barnett, *The Collapse of British Power* (Atlantic Highlands, NJ: Humanities Press International, 1986) is useful.

There is a large literature on each of the potential challengers listed in Chapter 3. For an optimistic earlier projection regarding Europe, see Mark Leonard, *Why Europe Will Run the 21st Century* (London: Fourth Estate, 2005), and for a more downbeat current description, see Jan Zielonka, *Is the EU Doomed?* (Cambridge: Polity, 2014.) On Japan, an early optimistic account is Ezra Vogel's *Japan as Number One: Lessons for America* (Cambridge, MA: Harvard University Press, 1979), and a current description is Sheila Smith, *Japan's New Politics and the US–Japan Alliance* (New York: Council on Foreign Relations, 2014). On Russia, see Anders Aslund, Sergei Guriev, and Andrew Kuchins, *Russia After the Global Economic Crisis* (Washington, DC: Peterson Institute, 2010), while Angela E. Stent offers a sober account in *The Limits of Partnership: US–Russian Relations in the Twenty-First Century* (Princeton: Princeton University Press, 2014). On India, see Vijay Joshi, "Economic resurgence, lopsided reform, and jobless growth," in Anthony Heath and Roger Jeffrey, eds., *Diversity and Change in Modern India: Economic, Social and Political Approaches* (Oxford: Oxford University Press, 2010). For Brazil, former president Fernando Enrique Cardoso provides a very readable account of its recent re-emergence in his memoir, *The Accidental President of Brazil: A Memoir* (New York: Public Affairs, 2006). A more complete history is provided in Thomas Skidmore, *Brazil: Five Centuries of Change* (Oxford:

Further Reading

Oxford University Press, 1999). Relations among Japan, India, and China are described well in Bill Emmott, *Rivals: How the Power Struggle Between China, India and Japan Will Shape Our Next Decade* (New York: Harcourt, 2008).

On China (discussed in Chapter 4), Martin Jacques provides a somewhat breathless account of *When China Rules the World: The End of the Western World and the Birth of a New Global Order* (New York: Penguin, 2009), which Jonathan Fenby counters with his more realistic assessment, *Will China Dominate the 21st Century* (Cambridge: Polity, 2014). A balanced account of the various dimensions of Chinese power can be found in David Shambaugh, *China Goes Global: The Partial Power* (Oxford: Oxford University Press, 2013). For an understanding of modern China's relations with the world, see Odd Arne Westad, *Restless Empire: China and the World Since 1750* (New York: Basic Books, 2012). James Steinberg and Michael O'Hanlon provide a good description of current relations between China and the United States in *Strategic Reassurance and Resolve: US–China Relations in the Twenty-First Century* (Princeton: Princeton University Press, 2014). Robert D. Kaplan describes some of the dangerous maritime issues involving China in *Asia's Cauldron: The South China Sea and the End of a Stable Pacific* (New York: Random House, 2014).

The question of American decline addressed in Chapter 5 has spawned a considerable literature of varying worth. Paul Kennedy's *Rise and Fall of the Great Powers* (cited above) posed the declinist position well in 1987, to which

Further Reading

I responded with *Bound to Lead: The Changing Nature of American Power* (New York: Basic Books, 1990.) More recently, the declinist view has been presented by Gideon Rachman, "Think again: American decline," *Foreign Policy*, January 2011; Charles Kupchan, "The decline of the West: Why America must prepare for the end of dominance," *The Atlantic*, March 2012; and Edward Luce, *Time to Start Thinking: America in the Age of Descent* (Bedford Park, IL: Atlantic Press, 2012) Optimistic views are offered by George Friedman, *The Next 100 Years: A Forecast for the 21st Century* (New York: Doubleday, 2009); Joseph Joffee, *The Myth of America's Decline* (New York: Norton, 2014); Robert Kagan, *The World America Made* (New York: Knopf, 2012) and Bruce Jones, *Still Ours to Lead* (Washington, DC: Brookings, 2014). Stephen G. Brooks and William Wohlforth make the case for continuing unipolarity in *World Out of Balance: International Relations and the Challenge of American Primacy* (Princeton: Princeton University Press, 2009). Nuno Monteiro presents *The Theory of Unilateral Politics* (New York: Cambridge University Press, 2014).

In relation to Chapter 6, I describe the diffusion of power, particularly cyber power, in my book *The Future of Power* (New York: Public Affairs, 2011). Moises Naim makes a similar case in *The End of Power* (New York: Basic Books, 2013). Charles Kupchan takes a more extreme view in *No-One's World: The West, the Rising Rest, and the Coming Global Turn* (New York: Oxford University Press, 2012). Ian Bremmer presents *Every Nation for Itself: Winners and Losers in a*

G-Zero World (New York: Penguin, 2012.) Anne Marie Slaughter describes the growing importance of networks in *A New World Order* (Princeton: Princeton University Press, 2004), and Fareed Zakaria warned about the rise of the rest in *The Post-American World* (New York: Norton, 2008). For a projection of the world in 2030, look at Office of the Director of National Intelligence, *Global Trends 2030: Alternative Worlds* (Washington, DC, 2012).

Finally, to follow up some of the issues in the conclusions, there is a deluge of books on American foreign policy, many with recommendations for the future. Michael Mandelbaum presents *The Case for Goliath* (New York: Public Affairs, 2005), while Andrew Bacevic presents a skeptical view of American policy in *The Limits of Power: The End of American Exceptionalism* (New York: Henry Holt, 2009). Richard Haass makes a case in *Foreign Policy Begins at Home: The Case for Putting America's House in Order* (New York: Basic Books), while Stephen Sestanovich describes the oscillation of American policy between periods of maximalism and retrenchment in *Maximalist* (New York: Knopf, 2014).

Notes

Chapter 1 The Creation of the American Century

1 Lester Thurow, *The Zero Sum Solution* (New York: Simon & Schuster, 1985), p. 67.
2 Kenneth Waltz, cited in Nuno P. Monteiro, *Theory of Unipolar Politics* (New York: Cambridge University Press, 2014), p. 29.
3 Herbert Block, *The Planetary Product in 1980* (Washington, DC: Department of State, 1981), p. 74; Simon Kuznets, *Economic Growth and Structure* (New York: W.W. Norton, 1965), p. 144.
4 Chris Giles, "China to overtake US as top economic power this year," *Financial Times*, April 30, 2014.
5 "Balance of power" is used to refer both to the distribution of power resources – military, economic, soft – among states, and to the policy of states acting to prevent any one country becoming so powerful as to pose a threat to the independence of others.
6 Michael Lind, "The American Century is over: How

our country went down in a blaze of shame," *Salon*, July 12, 2014.

7 Alan Brinkley, *The Publisher: Henry Luce and His American Century* (New York: Knopf, 2010), pp. 266–273.

8 Charles Kupchan, *No-One's World: The West, the Rising Rest, and the Coming Global Turn* (New York: Oxford University Press, 2012), p. 84.

9 See Paul Kennedy, *The Rise and Fall of the Great Powers: Economic Change and Military Conflict Among the Great Powers from 1500 to 2000* (New York: Random House, 1987), pp. 154, 203. See also Bruce Russett, "The mysterious case of vanishing hegemony," *International Organization* 39, Spring 1985, p. 212.

10 Corelli Barnett, *The Collapse of British Power* (Atlantic Highlands, NJ: Humanities Press International, 1986), p. 72.

11 Richard Ned Lebow and Benjamin Valentino, "Lost in transition: A critical analysis of power transition theory," *International Relations* 23/2, 2009, p. 389.

12 G. John Ikenberry, *Liberal Order and Imperial Ambition* (Cambridge: Polity, 2006) p. 14.

13 Robert O. Keohane, *After Hegemony: Cooperation and Discord in the World Political Economy* (Princeton: Princeton University Press, 1984).

14 Amitav Acharya, *The End of American World Order* (Cambridge: Polity, 2014).

15 Henry Kissinger, *World Order* (New York: Penguin, 2014), p. 2.

16 Acharya, *The End of American World Order*, p. 11.

17 Noam Chomsky, "Losing the world: American decline in perspective, part 1," *Guardian*, February 14, 2012.

Chapter 2 American Decline?

1 George Modelski, *Long Cycles in World Politics* (Seattle: University of Washington Press, 1987).

2 Immanuel Wallerstein, *The Politics of the World Economy* (New York: Cambridge University Press, 1984,) p. 41.

3 Charles Dickens, quoted in David Whitman, *The Optimism Gap: The I'm OK – They're Not Syndrome and the Myth of American Decline* (New York: Walker, 1998), p. 85.

4 Samuel P. Huntington, "The US – Decline or Renewal?" *Foreign Affairs* 67, Winter 1988/9, p. 95.

5 *America's Place in the World 2013* (Washington, DC: Pew Research Center, 2013), pp. 4, 10.

6 James Fallows, "How America can rise again," *The Atlantic*, January/February 2010.

Chapter 3 Challengers and Relative Decline

1 Nicolas Serge, *Creative Industries and Culture-Based Economy – Creative Industries and Cultural Diplomacy* (Berlin: Institute for Cultural Diplomacy, 2013).

2 *From International Blockbusters to National Hits: Analysis of the 2010 UIS Survey on Feature Film*

Statistics (Montreal: UNESCO Institute for Statistics, 2012), pp. 5–8.

3 Mikhail Gorbachev, speech to Soviet writers, quoted in "Gorbachev on the future: 'We will not give in,'" *New York Times*, December 22, 1986.

4 Clifford J. Levy, "Russian president calls for nation to modernize," *New York Times*, November 13, 2009.

5 "The engineering gap," *The Economist*, January 30, 2010, p. 76.

6 McKinsey Global Institute, *Connecting Brazil to the World: A Path to Inclusive Growth* (McKinsey & Company, May 2014), p. 3.

7 "Getting it together at last: A special report on business and finance in Brazil," *The Economist*, November 14, 2009, pp. 5, 18.

8 Robert Fogel, "$123,000,000,000,000," *Foreign Policy*, January 4, 2010, p. 70.

9 Gideon Rachman, "Think Again: American Decline," *Foreign Policy*, January 2, 2011.

Chapter 4 The Rise of China

1 Niall Ferguson, quoted in Jonathan Fenby, *Will China Dominate the 21st Century?* (Cambridge: Polity, 2014), p. 13. See also Martin Jacques, *When China Rules the World* (New York: Penguin, 2009).

2 "American Opinion," *Wall Street Journal*, September 16, 1999, p. A9.

3 See Joseph Nye, "As China rises, must others bow?" *The Economist*, June 27, 1998, p. 23.

4 John Mearsheimer, *The Tragedy of Great Power Politics* (New York, W.W. Norton, 2001), p. 4.

5 Ingrid d'Hooghe, *The Limits of China's Soft Power in Europe: Beijing's Public Diplomacy Puzzle* (The Hague: Netherlands Institute of International Relations, 2010).

6 Thucydides, *History of the Peloponnesian War* (London: Penguin, 1972), p. 62.

7 Fenby, *Will China Dominate the 21st Century?*, p. 26.

8 "Living up to the title," *Beijing Review*, May 22, 2014, p. 2; Daniel Gross, "Yes we can still market: Why US brands remain the world's most valuable," *The Daily Beast*, June 1, 2014.

9 Alexandra Raphel, "American economic power in decline? Rethinking the data in the context of globalization," *Journalist's Resource*, February 11, 2014.

10 Neil Irwin, "This one number explains how China is taking over the world," *Washington Post.com*, December 3, 2013; "The once and future currency," *The Economist*, March 8, 2014, p. 80.

11 *South Reviews* editorial, reprinted in *Beijing Review*, March 27, 2014, p. 10.

12 Toshiya Tsugami, "The future growth of China and security in East Asia," paper presented to SPF–CSIS Joint Commission on the US–Japan Alliance, June 24, 2013.

13 Sam Roberts, "In 2025, India to pass China in population, US estimates," *New York Times*, December 16, 2009.

14 Richard McGregor, *The Party: The Secret World*

of China's Communist Rulers (New York: Harper Collins, 2010), p. 30.

15 James Steinberg and Michael O'Hanlon, *Strategic Reassurance and Resolve: US–China Relations in the Twenty-First Century* (Princeton: Princeton University Press, 2014), pp. 93, 184.

16 Evan Braden Montgomery, "Contested primacy in the Western Pacific," *International Security* 38, Spring 2014, pp. 115–149.

17 "Sun Tzu and the art of soft power," *The Economist*, December 17, 2011.

18 Jacques, *When China Rules the World*, p. 12.

19 David C. Kang, "Hierarchy in Asian international relations: 1300–1900," *Asian Security*, 1/1, 2005, pp. 53–79. See also Stefan Halper, *The Beijing Consensus: How China's Authoritarian Model Will Dominate the Twenty-First Century* (New York: Basic Books, 2010).

20 John Ikenberry, "The rise of China and the future of the West," *Foreign Affairs* 87/1, January/February 2008, pp. 23–38.

21 Robert Kagan, "What China knows that we don't: The case for a new strategy of containment," *The Weekly Standard*, January 20, 1997. Robert Kaplan, *Asia's Cauldron: The South China Sea and the End of a Stable Pacific* (New York: Random House, 2014).

22 Steinberg and O'Hanlon, *Strategic Reassurance and Resolve*, p. 20.

23 For a detailed analysis, see Bill Emmott, *Rivals: How the Power Struggle Between China, India and Japan*

Will Shape Our Next Decade (New York: Harcourt, 2008).

24 Yan Xuetong, "How China can defeat America," *New York Times*, November 21, 2011.

25 Fareed Zakaria, "Obama needs to lead with feeling," *Washington Post*, May 8, 2014.

26 Carla Norrlof and Simon Reich, "What would Kindleberger say: The US and China as world economic leaders and stabilizers," unpublished paper, 2014.

Chapter 5 Absolute Decline: Is America Like Rome?

1 Cullen Murphy, *Are We Rome? The Fall of an Empire and the Fate of America* (New York: Mariner Books, 2007).

2 Paul Kennedy, *The Rise and Fall of the Great Powers: Economic Change and Military Conflict Among the Great Powers from 1500 to 2000* (New York: Random House, 1987).

3 Of course, there were many more causes of this complex phenomenon. See Ramsay MacMullen, *Corruption and the Decline of Rome* (New Haven: Yale University Press, 1988).

4 See Nicholas Kristof, "We're not no. 1! We're not no. 1!" *New York Times*, April 3, 2014.

5 "The jobs machine," *The Economist*, April 13, 2013.

6 Klaus Schwab and Xavier Sala-i-Martin, *The Global Competitiveness Report 2013–14* (Davos: World Economic Forum, 2013). Niall Ferguson, "How

America lost its way," *Wall Street Journal*, June 7, 2013.

7 *Technically Recoverable Shale Oil and Shale Gas Resources: An Assessment of 137 Shale Formations in 41 Countries Outside the United States* (Washington, DC: US Energy Information Agency, 2013), p. 3.

8 *2014 Global R&D Funding Forecast* (Columbus: Batelle Memorial Institute, 2014).

9 *US Patent Statistics Chart, Calendar Years 1963–2013* (Washington, DC: The United States Patent and Trademark Office).

10 For a more optimistic view of American savings, see Richard N. Cooper, "Global imbalances: Globalization, demography, and sustainability," *Journal of Economic Perspectives* 22, Summer 2008, p. 95.

11 Niall Ferguson, "An empire at risk," *Newsweek*, December 7, 2009, p. 28; and "A Greek crisis is coming to America," *Financial Times*, February 11, 2010. See also, Francis Warnock, "How dangerous is US government debt? The risk of a sudden spike in US interest rates," Council on Foreign Relations Report, June 2010; available at: http://www.cfr.org/pub lication/22408/how_dangerous_is_us_government_ debt.html.

12 Institute of Higher Education of Shanghai Jiao Tong University, "Academic ranking of the world universities – 2009"; available at: http://www.arwu.org/ ARWU2009.jsp.

13 "Are higher and lower performing students making

gains?" *The Nation's Report Card* (Washington, DC: National Center for Education Statistics, US Department of Education, 2013); available at: http://www.nationsreportcard.gov/reading_math_2013/#/gains-percentiles.

14 Viktória Kis and Simon Field, *Time for the US to Reskill? What the Survey of Adult Skills Says* (Washington, DC: Organization for Economic Cooperation and Development, 2013), p. 12.

15 Sam Dillon, "Many nations passing US in education, expert says," *New York Times*, March 10, 2010.

16 "Gini in the bottle," *The Economist*, November 26, 2013.

17 Eduardo Porter, "A relentless widening of disparity in wealth," *New York Times*, March 12, 2014; "Class in America: Mobility measured, *The Economist*, February 1, 2014; Lawrence Summers, "US inequality goes beyond dollars and cents," *Washington Post*, June 8, 2014.

18 Francis Fukuyama, "American power is waning because Washington won't stop quarreling," *The New Republic*, March 10, 2014.

19 Sarah Binder, "Polarized we govern?" Washington, DC, Brookings Center for Effective Public Management, May 2014, p. 18.

20 Pew Research Center for the People and the Press, "Political polarization in the American public," June 12, 2014.

21 Henry Kissinger, "America at the apex," *The National Interest*, Summer 2001, p. 15.

22 Hart-Teeter Poll for the Council of Excellence in

Government, reported in the *Washington Post*, March 24, 1997. See also Seymour Martin Lipset and William Schneider, *The Confidence Gap* (Baltimore: Johns Hopkins University Press, 1987) and Jeffrey Jones, "Trust in Government Remains Low," *Gallup*, September 18, 2008.

23 Harris Poll, 1966–2011, "Confidence in Congress and Supreme Court drops to lowest level in many years," May 18, 2011.

24 Joseph S. Nye, Philip Zelikow, and David King, eds, *Why People Don't Trust Government* (Cambridge, MA: Harvard University Press, 1996).

25 Department of the Treasury, *Update on Reducing the Federal Tax Gap and Improving Voluntary Compliance* (Washington, DC: July 8, 2009). "Employment tax evasion", *Criminal Investigation Management Information System* (Washington, DC: Internal Revenue Service, October 2013).

26 The World Bank, *Governance Matters 2009: Worldwide Governance Indicators, 1996–2008* (Washington, DC: The World Bank, 2009).

27 Steven Holmes, "Defying forecasts, census response ends declining trend," *New York Times*, September 20, 2000; Sam Roberts, "1 in 3 Americans failed to return census forms," *New York Times*, April 17, 2010.

28 Robert Putnam, *Bowling Alone: The Collapse and Revival of American Community* (New York: Simon & Schuster, 2000); see also *Better Together: Restoring the American Community* (New York: Simon & Schuster, 2003).

29 "What's wrong in Washington," *The Economist*, February 29, 2010, p. 11.
30 David Frum, "Crashing the party," *Foreign Affairs* 93/5, September/October 2014, p. 46.

Chapter 6 Power Shifts and Global Complexity

1 For a full description, see Joseph Nye, *The Future of Power* (New York: Public Affairs, 2011).
2 Niall Ferguson, "Networks and hierarchies," *The American Interest*, June 2014.
3 Anne-Marie Slaughter, "America's edge", *Foreign Affairs*, January/February 2009.
4 Randall Schweller, 'Emerging powers in an age of disorder," *Global Governance* 17, 2011, p. 286. See also Charles Kupchan, *No-One's World: The West, the Rising Rest, and the Coming Global Turn* (New York: Oxford University Press, 2012).
5 Office of the Director of National Intelligence, *Global Trends 2030: Alternative Worlds* (Washington, DC, 2012).
6 Robert Kagan, *The World America Made* (New York: Knopf, 2012), p. 105.
7 International Monetary Fund, *World Economic Outlook Database, April 2012* (Washington, DC: IMF, 2013).
8 Jim O'Neill and Alessio Terzi, "Changing trade patterns, unchanging European and global governance," Brussels, Bruegel Working Paper, February 2014, p. 3.
9 See Peter Zeihan, *The Accidental Superpower: The Next Generation of American Pre-eminence and*

the Coming Global Disorder (New York: Hachette, 2014).

10 Jonathan Kirshner, *American Power After the Financial Crisis* (Ithaca: Cornell University Press, 2014), p. 143.

11 Michael Mandelbaum, *The Case for Goliath* (New York: Public Affairs, 2005), p. 226.

12 Robert O. Keohane and Joseph S. Nye, "Between centralization and fragmentation: The club model of multilateral cooperation and problems of democratic legitimacy," John F. Kennedy School of Government, Harvard University, Faculty Research Working Paper Series, RWP01-004 (February 2001).

13 See J. S. Nye, "Maintaining the non-proliferation regime," *International Organization*, Winter 1981, pp. 15–38.

14 "Market value of the largest internet companies worldwide as of May 2013," Statista; available at: http://www.statista.com/statistics/277483/market-value-of-the-largest-internet-companies-worldwide/. Note: Yahoo and Yahoo-Japan have been treated as one entity for the purposes of company rankings.

15 Jonathan Zittrain, "No Barack Obama isn't handing control of the internet over to China," *The New Republic* 224, March 24, 2014.

16 Richard J. Danzig, *Surviving on a Diet of Poisoned Fruit: Reducing the National Security Risks of America's Cyber Dependencies* (Washington, DC: Center for New American Security, 2014), p. 25.

17 Moises Naim, *The End of Power* (New York: Basic Books, 2013), p. 52.

327.73 NYE

18 Quoted in Nathan Gardels, "Governance after the end of power," *New Perspectives Quarterly*, Summer 2013, p. 4.

19 David Brooks, "The leaderless doctrine," *New York Times*, March 14, 2014.

Chapter 7 Conclusions

1 George Friedman, *The Next 100 Years: A Forecast for the 21st Century* (New York: Doubleday, 2009), p. 18.

2 Lawrence Freedman, "A subversive on a hill," *The National Interest*, May/June 2009, p. 39.

3 Stephen Sestanovich, *Maximalist* (New York: Knopf, 2014).

4 David Ignatius, "Claims of US weakness and retreat of US power are unfounded," *Washington Post*, June 4, 2014.

5 Mackubin Thomas Owens, "Obama chooses national decline," *National Review Online*, February 26, 2014; William Kristol, "Superpower once lived here," *Weekly Standard*, April 7, 2014, p. 7.

6 Fareed Zakaria, "The perils of leaning forward," *The Washington Post*, June 5, 2014.

7 Robert Zoellick, "A presidency of missed opportunities," *Wall Street Journal*, August 10, 2014.

LIBRARY